SADLIER-OXFORD

W9-AVR-220

Vocabulary Workshop

Enhanced Edition

The classic program for:

- *developing* and *enhancing* vocabulary resources

- *promoting* more effective communication in today's world

- *improving* vocabulary skills assessed on standardized and/or college-admission tests

By
Jerome Shostak

Sadlier-Oxford

A Division of William H. Sadlier, Inc.
9 Pine Street
New York, New York 10005-1002
1-800-221-5175

Contents

Copyright © 1996 by
Sadlier-Oxford,
A Division of
William H. Sadlier, Inc.

ISBN: 0-8215-0608-0
89/9

Home Office: 9 Pine Street
New York, NY 10005-1002
1-800-221-5175

Foreword

For close to five decades VOCABULARY WORKSHOP has been a highly successful tool for guiding and stimulating systematic vocabulary growth for students. It has also been extremely valuable for preparing students to take the types of standardized vocabulary tests commonly used to assess grade placement, competence for graduation, and/or college readiness. The *Enhanced Edition* has faithfully maintained those features that have made the program so beneficial in these two areas, while introducing new elements to keep abreast of changing times and changing standardized-test procedures, particularly the SAT. The features that make VOCABULARY WORKSHOP so valuable include:

Word List
Each book contains 300 or more basic words, selected on the basis of:
- currency in present-day usage
- frequency on recognized vocabulary lists
- applicability to standardized tests
- current grade-placement research

Units
The words in each book are organized around 15 short, stimulating *Units* featuring:
- pronunciation and parts of speech
New! • definitions—fuller treatment in the *Enhanced Edition*
- synonyms and antonyms
- usage (one phrase and two sentences)

Reviews
Five *Reviews* highlight and reinforce the work of the units through challenging exercises involving:
New! • shades of meaning (SAT-type critical-thinking exercise)
- definitions
- synonyms and antonyms
- analogies
- sentence completions
- word families

Cumulative Reviews
Four *Cumulative Reviews* utilize standardized testing techniques to provide ongoing assessment of word mastery, all involving SAT-type critical-thinking skills. Here the exercises revolve around
New! • shades of meaning • analogies • two-word completions

Additional Features
- A *Diagnostic Test* provides ready assessment of student needs at the outset of the term.
- The *Vocabulary of Vocabulary* reviews terms and concepts needed for effective word study.
- The *Final Mastery Test* provides end-of-term assessment of student achievement.
- *Building with Word Roots* introduces the study of etymology.
- *Enhancing Your Vocabulary,* Levels F through H, introduces students to the study of word clusters.
New! • *Working with Parts of Speech,* Levels F through H, provides further work with word clusters and introduces 50 new words per level.

Ancillary Materials
- An *Answer Key* for each level supplies answers to all materials in the student text.
- A *Series Teacher's Guide* provides a thorough overview of the features in each level, along with tips for using them effectively.
- The *Supplementary Testing Program: Cycle One, Cycle Two* provide two complete programs of separate and different testing materials for each level, so testing can be varied. A *Combined Answer Key* for each level is also available.
- The SAT-type *TEST PREP Blackline Masters* for each level provide further testing materials designed to help students prepare for SAT-type standardized tests.
- An *Interactive Audio Pronunciation Program* is also available for each level.

Pronunciation Key

The pronunciation is indicated for every basic word introduced in this book. The symbols used for this purpose, as listed below, are similar to those appearing in most standard dictionaries of recent vintage. The author has consulted a large number of dictionaries for this purpose but has relied primarily on *Webster's Third New International Dictionary* and *The Random House Dictionary of the English Language (Unabridged)*.

There are, of course, many English words for which two (or more) pronunciations are commonly accepted. In virtually all cases where such words occur in this book, the author has sought to make things easier for the student by giving just one pronunciation. The only significant exception occurs when the pronunciation changes in accordance with a shift in the part of speech. Thus we would indicate that *project* in the verb form is pronounced prə 'jekt, and in the noun form, 'präj ekt.

It is believed that these relatively simple pronunciation guides will be readily usable by the student. It should be emphasized, however, that the *best* way to learn the pronunciation of a word is to listen to and imitate an educated speaker.

Vowels						
$\bar{a}$	lake	e	stress	ü	loot, new
a	mat	$\bar{\imath}$	knife	u̇	foot, pull
â	care	i	sit	ə	rug, broken
ä	bark, bottle	$\bar{o}$	flow	ər	bird, better
au̇	doubt	ô	all, cord		
ē	beat, wordy	oi	oil		

Consonants						
ch	child, lecture	s	cellar	wh	what
g	give	sh	shun	y	yearn
j	gentle, bridge	th	thank	z	is
ŋ	sing	th	those	zh	measure

All other consonants are sounded as in the alphabet.

Stress   The accent mark *precedes* the syllable receiving the major stress: en 'rich

Parts of Speech				
adj.	adjective	n.	noun
adv.	adverb	part.	participle
cap.	capital letter	pl.	plural
f.	feminine	prep.	preposition
int.	interjection	trans.	transitive
intrans.	intransitive	v.	verb

The Vocabulary of Vocabulary

In order to be able to discuss words as words, you must become familiar with some special terms used commonly in the study of vocabulary.

Synonyms, Antonyms, Homonyms

I. Synonyms

A *synonym* is a word that is similar in meaning to another word.

EXAMPLES:

cheerful—glad   select—choose
attempt—try   mercy—kindness

Exercises

*In each of the following groups, encircle the word that is most nearly **the same** in meaning as the first word in **boldface type.***

1. praise
a. flattery
b. ability
c. excitement
d. sight

2. halt
a. cry
b. begin
c. hold
d. stop

3. salary
a. cost
b. pay
c. check
d. order

4. perfect
a. hold
b. whole
c. holy
d. wholesome

5. pleasant
a. tall
b. mighty
c. agreeable
d. noisy

6. quarrel
a. conflict
b. doubt
c. worry
d. injury

7. thief
a. lieutenant
b. follower
c. burglar
d. chief

8. careful
a. experienced
b. brave
c. heroic
d. cautious

II. Antonyms

An *antonym* is a word that is opposite in meaning to another word.

EXAMPLES:

generous—stingy   love—hate
give—take   swift—slow

Exercises

*In each of the following groups, encircle the word that is most nearly the **opposite** in meaning to the word in **boldface type.***

1. graceful
a. good
b. awkward
c. gracious
d. polite

2. cheerful
a. loud
b. soft
c. sad
d. silent

3. conceal
a. burn
b. hide
c. reveal
d. skin

4. certain
a. real
b. guilty
c. dark
d. questionable

5. sorrow
a. distress
b. fear
c. joy
d. poverty

6. gentle
a. violent
b. breezy
c. close
d. distant

7. glorious
a. patriotic
b. shameful
c. dangerous
d. hard

8. linger
a. hasten
b. fish
c. eat
d. study

III. Homonyms

A *homonym* is a word having the same (or almost the same) pronunciation as another word but a different meaning and a different spelling.

EXAMPLES:

be—bee   steak—stake   right—write

Exercises   *In each of the following sentences, encircle in the parentheses the **homonym** that correctly completes the meaning.*

1. His admirers call him a man of (**steel, steal**).
2. What will tomorrow's (**weather, whether**) be?
3. (**Witch, Which**) one did you choose?
4. All I wanted was a slice of (**plane, plain**) cake.
5. I bought that jacket during the recent (**sail, sale**).
6. It was a (**scene, seen**) I shall never forget.
7. It was the (**right, rite**) thing to do.
8. Put the cleaned fish in the (**pail, pale**).
9. How long did Queen Elizabeth I (**rain, reign**)?
10. Where can I (**find, fined**) a replacement?

Parts of a Word

Prefixes   A *prefix* is a syllable or syllables placed at the beginning of a word.

EXAMPLES: *ab- dis- anti- com-*

Suffixes   A *suffix* is a syllable or syllables placed at the end of a word.

EXAMPLES: *-or -ary -(t)ion*

Roots   A *root* or *base* is the main part of the word to which prefixes and suffixes may be added.

EXAMPLES: *-scrib- -cept- -pend-*

NOTE: The word *affix* is sometimes used to identify either a prefix or a suffix. Thus, an affix may be placed before or after the root or base of a word.

Exercises   *Divide each of the following words into its prefix, root, and suffix. Some of the words may lack a prefix, a suffix, or both. The first word has been done for you.*

Word	Prefix	Root	Suffix
1. **expensive**	ex	pens	ive
2. **container**	_____	_____	_____
3. **reliable**	_____	_____	_____
4. **mindful**	_____	_____	_____
5. **disarm**	_____	_____	_____
6. **confusion**	_____	_____	_____
7. **retention**	_____	_____	_____
8. **complainer**	_____	_____	_____

9. defender _____ _____ _____

10. description _____ _____ _____

Denotation and Connotation

Denotation The _denotation_ of a word is its specific dictionary definition.

Examples:

Word	Denotation
humane	kindly and merciful
braggart	boastful person
search	look for

Connotation The _connotation_ of a word is its _tone_—that is, the emotions or associations it normally arouses in people using, hearing, or reading it. Depending on what these feelings are, the connotation of a word may be _favorable (positive)_ or _unfavorable (pejorative)._ A word that does not normally arouse strong emotions of any kind has a _neutral_ connotation.

Examples:

Word	Connotation
humane	favorable
braggart	unfavorable
search	neutral

Exercises In the space provided, label the connotation of each of the following words **F** for "favorable," **U** for "unfavorable," or **N** for "neutral."

_____ **1.** radiant   _____ **5.** fickle   _____ **9.** malignant

_____ **2.** grovel   _____ **6.** poise   _____ **10.** coincide

_____ **3.** luster   _____ **7.** narrative   _____ **11.** deft

_____ **4.** despot   _____ **8.** dingy   _____ **12.** mutual

Literal and Figurative Usage

Literal Usage When a word is being used in a _literal_ sense, it is being employed in its strict (or primary) dictionary meaning in a situation (or _context_) that "makes sense" from a purely logical point of view.

Example: On our hike we picked berries, _mushrooms,_ and other wild plants.

Figurative Usage Sometimes words are used in a symbolic or nonliteral way in situations that do not "make sense" from a purely logical point of view. We call this nonliteral or "extended" application of a word a _figurative_ or _metaphorical_ usage.

Example: Almost overnight, a minor border incident _mushroomed_ into a major international crisis.

4

Exercises In the space provided, write **L** for "literal" or **F** for "figurative" next to each of the following sentences to show how the italicized word is being used.

_____ **1.** Fireworks displays on the Fourth of July usually include *skyrockets*, Roman candles, and other spectacular illuminations.

_____ **2.** During a period of sharp inflation, prices on consumer goods *skyrocket* at an alarming rate.

_____ **3.** Noah and his family were the only human beings who survived the great *deluge* that, according to the Bible, once engulfed the earth.

_____ **4.** Every spring, companies all over the country are *deluged* with mail from college students looking for summer employment.

_____ **5.** When she was suddenly cut adrift from the home and family that had buoyed her up for so long, she quite understandably felt all *at sea*.

_____ **6.** When he was a young man, my father joined the navy and went *to sea*.

Analogies

An *analogy* is a comparison. For example, we can draw an analogy between the human eye and a camera.

In examinations you may be asked to find the relationship between two words. Then to show that you understand the relationship, you are asked to choose another pair of words that show the same type of relationship.

Example: **elm** is to **tree** as
a. hand is to glove
b. bison is to animal
c. ship is to ocean
d. fork is to machine

Since an elm is a kind of tree, the correct answer is *b, bison is to animal*. A bison, of course, is a kind of animal.

Exercises Encircle the item that best completes each analogy.

1. small is to **tiny** as
a. cold is to frigid
b. red is to angry
c. dull is to colorful
d. cheap is to expensive

2. rung is to **ladder** as
a. pot is to kettle
b. roof is to house
c. match is to lighter
d. step is to staircase

3. neat is to **tidy** as
a. normal is to unusual
b. gigantic is to colossal
c. deep is to dry
d. tall is to short

4. hammer is to **tool** as
a. soprano is to opera
b. tree is to forest
c. typewriter is to machine
d. horse is to vehicle

5. practice is to **perfect** as
a. interest is to bored
b. experience is to talented
c. study is to knowledgeable ·
d. wealth is to wise

6. veterinarian is to **animals** as
a. druggist is to vagrants
b. lawyer is to fees
c. theologian is to angels
d. warden is to prisoners

7. visible is to **see** as
a. edible is to taste
b. audible is to hear
c. flammable is to flood
d. movable is to control

8. ship is to **nautical** as
a. helicopter is to lunar
b. bicycle is to marine
c. automobile is to terrestrial
d. skateboard is to underground

9. fugitive is to **flee** as
a. spectator is to observe
b. doctor is to operate
c. showoff is to conceal
d. judge is to prosecute

10. kindle is to **extinguish** as
a. live is to dwell
b. study is to examine
c. listen is to learn
d. start is to stop

Context Clues

When you do the various word-omission exercises in this book, look for *context clues* built right into the passage to guide you to the correct answer.

Restatement Clues

A *restatement clue* consists of a synonym for, or a definition of, a missing word.

Example:

When I told my landlord that I was planning to _____ my apartment, he didn't seem too unhappy to see me <u>depart</u>.

a. clean   (b.) vacate   c. furnish   d. redecorate

Contrast Clues

A *contrast clue* consists of an antonym for, or a phrase that means the opposite of, a missing word.

Example:

Though some of my <u>classmates</u> are decidedly <u>skinny</u>, others are definitely (**thin,** (**overweight**)).

Inference Clues

An *inference clue* implies but does not directly state the meaning of a missing word.

Example:

"Only a <u>trial</u> in a bona fide court of law can <u>determine</u> the _____ of the <u>charges</u> leveled at <u>my client</u>," the _____ said.

a. effect . . . prosecutor   (c.) validity . . . defense attorney
b. relevance . . . judge   d. appropriateness . . . juror

Exercises

Use context clues to choose the word or words that complete each of the following sentences.

1. Though I was brought up in a completely (**rural, urban**) environment, life in the big city suits me to a tee.

2. People with _____ ideas are always thinking up new and different things to do, or say, or make.

   a. vague   b. simple   c. old-fashioned   d. original

3. Because a medieval castle was primarily a fortress, scholars point out that it was built more for _____ than for _____ .

   a. decoration . . . usefulness
   b. defense . . . comfort
   c. aggression . . . protection
   d. pageantry . . . style

Diagnostic Test

This test contains a sampling of the words that are to be found in the exercises in this Vocabulary Workshop. It will give you an idea of the types and levels of the words to be studied. When you have completed all the units, the Final Mastery Test at the end of the book will assess what you have learned. By comparing your results on the Final Mastery Test with your results on the Diagnostic Test below, you will be able to judge your progress.

Synonyms   *In each of the following groups, encircle the word or phrase that most nearly expresses the meaning of the word in* **boldface type** *in the introductory phrase.*

1. choose an appropriate **excerpt**
a. topic   b. title   c. selection   d. leader

2. surrounded by **servile** followers
a. cringing   b. patriotic   c. brave   d. faithful

3. the **plaudits** of the people
a. wishes   b. complaints   c. praises   d. fears

4. **preclude** failure
a. anticipate   b. prevent   c. cause   d. reveal

5. handle **gingerly**
a. quickly   b. successfully   c. too late   d. cautiously

6. an **avowed** enemy
a. deadly   b. weak   c. declared   d. defeated

7. **oblique** glances
a. angry   b. loving   c. longing   d. sideways

8. **garnish** a salad
a. eat   b. toss   c. prepare   d. decorate

9. **devoid** of pity
a. full   b. empty   c. result   d. cause

10. a **detriment** to success
a. doubt   b. aid   c. block   d. opening

11. **deface** public property
a. damage   b. sell   c. repair   d. steal

12. **solicitous** about our problems
a. talking   b. concerned   c. questioning   d. writing

13. become a **nonentity**
a. voter   b. leader   c. nobody   d. scholar

14. **peruse** the report
a. write   b. read   c. vote on   d. approve

15. a **plausible** excuse
a. reasonable   b. lengthy   c. angry   d. confused

16. have **ample** opportunity
a. little   b. rare   c. unusual   d. sufficient

17. write a **sequel**
a. letter   b. follow-up   c. novel   d. summary

18. facetious remarks
a. sensible   b. dull   c. interesting   d. humorous

19. a vague **premonition** of disaster
a. cause   b. rumor   c. echo   d. hunch

20. infiltrated enemy lines
a. destroyed   b. avoided   c. strengthened   d. penetrated

21. filled with **anguish**
a. distress   b. joy   c. patience   d. annoyance

22. the **acme** of success
a. cause   b. lack   c. cost   d. top

23. struck a **discordant** note in the proceedings
a. welcome   b. jarring   c. strange   d. sensible

24. convey our regrets
a. feel   b. carry   c. cause   d. soothe

25. a man whose deeds have been **vilified** by history
a. remembered   b. celebrated   c. badmouthed   d. ignored

26. perceptible changes
a. sudden   b. noticeable   c. painful   d. costly

27. plundered the treasury
a. set up   b. attacked   c. robbed   d. reformed

28. do her **stint**
a. share   b. best   c. worst   d. least

29. refuse to **capitulate**
a. ask   b. listen   c. surrender   d. cooperate

30. a **dire** result
a. favorable   b. dreadful   c. sensible   d. predictable

Antonyms   *In each of the following groups, encircle the word or expression that is most nearly **opposite** in meaning to the word in **boldface type** in the introductory phrase.*

31. negligent owners
a. overworked   b. elderly   c. responsible   d. happy-go-lucky

32. a group of **ramshackle** buildings
a. sturdy   b. ancient   c. battered   d. useless

33. tractable mules
a. strong   b. unmanageable   c. tame   d. hungry

34. outlandish behavior
a. weird   b. embarrassing   c. normal   d. rude

35. a **haughty** young man
a. clever   b. wealthy   c. angry   d. humble

36. inert officials
a. active   b. stupid   c. frightened   d. greedy

37. a **judicious** choice of words
a. sensible
b. cautious
c. sensitive
d. foolish

38. a very **volatile** situation
a. explosive
b. puzzling
c. stable
d. unusual

39. a **whimsical** account of her travels
a. lengthy
b. funny
c. humorless
d. short

40. new evidence that will **bolster** our case
a. improve
b. weaken
c. clinch
d. concern

41. increased the **enmity** between the two countries
a. friendship
b. trade
c. hostility
d. tourism

42. **excised** the meaningless sentence
a. wrote
b. inserted
c. questioned
d. ignored

43. was **rational** when he committed the crime
a. guilty
b. intelligent
c. responsible
d. insane

44. **upbraided** the children for what they had done
a. fined
b. praised
c. scolded
d. punished

45. tried to **minimize** my part in the victory
a. increase
b. ignore
c. reduce
d. match

46. **appease** a bully
a. satisfy
b. avoid
c. enrage
d. protect

47. a **cryptic** message
a. verbal
b. clear
c. lengthy
d. sad

48. a **skittish** driver
a. new
b. confident
c. careless
d. timid

49. **kindred** spirits
a. intoxicating
b. warlike
c. happy
d. unlike

50. **disgruntled** customers
a. satisfied
b. demanding
c. numerous
d. rich

Definitions

Note carefully the spelling, pronunciation, and definition of each of the following words. Then write the word in the blank space in the illustrative phrase following.

1. adage
('ad ij)

(n.) a proverb, wise saying

quote an old _____

2. bonanza
(bə 'nan zə)

(n.) a rich mass of ore in a mine; something very valuable, profitable, or rewarding; a source of wealth or prosperity; a very large amount

a box-office _____

3. churlish
('chər lish)

(adj.) lacking politeness or good manners; lacking sensitivity; difficult to work with or deal with; rude

annoyed by his _____ reply

4. citadel
('sit ə del)

(n.) a fortress that overlooks and protects a city; any strong or commanding place

the _____ that guarded Troy

5. collaborate
(kə 'lab ə rāt)

(v.) to work with, work together

_____ on a project

6. decree
(di 'krē)

(n.) an order having the force of law; (v.) to issue such an order; to command firmly or forcefully

a papal _____

7. discordant
(dis 'kôr dənt)

(adj.) disagreeable in sound, jarring; lacking in harmony, conflicting

struck a _____ note

8. evolve
(ē 'välv)

(v.) to develop gradually; to rise to a higher level

notes that _____ into a book

9. excerpt
('ek sərpt)

(n.) a passage taken from a book, article, etc.; (v.) to take such a passage; to quote

choose an _____ from the essay

10. grope
(grōp)

(v.) to feel about hesitantly with the hands; to search blindly and uncertainly

_____ in the dark for the light switch

11. hover
('həv ər)

(v.) to float or hang suspended over; to move back and forth uncertainly over or around

vultures _____ in the air

12. jostle
('jäs əl)

(v.) to make or force one's way by pushing or elbowing; to bump, shove, brush against; to vie for

_____ by other riders on the bus

13. laggard
('lag ərd)

(n.) a person who moves slowly or falls behind; (adj.) falling behind; slow to move, act, or respond

_____ in their payments

14. plaudits
('plô ditz)

(*pl. n.*) applause; enthusiastic praise or approval

accept the _____ of his fans

15. preclude
(prē 'klüd)

(*v.*) to make impossible, prevent, shut out

_____ a second chance

16. revert
(rē 'vərt)

(*v.*) to return, go back

_____ to its original owner

17. rubble
('rəb əl)

(*n.*) broken stone or bricks; ruins

searched among the _____

18. servile
('sər vīl)

(*adj.*) of or relating to a slave; behaving like or suitable for a slave or a servant, menial; lacking spirit or independence, abjectly submissive

disgusted by such _____ flattery

19. vigil
('vij əl)

(*n.*) a watch, especially at night; any period of watchful attention

take part in the all-night _____

20. wrangle
('raŋ gəl)

(*v.*) to quarrel or argue in a noisy, angry way; to obtain by argument; to herd; (*n.*) a noisy quarrel

a nasty _____ with the clerk

Completing the Sentence

From the words for this unit, choose the one that best completes each of the following sentences. Write the word in the space provided.

1. The cafeteria line was so crowded that I was _____ past the desserts before I could take one.

2. The swiftest members of the herd escaped the trappers' nets, but the _____ were caught.

3. Let me read aloud a few _____ from the newspaper review of the new movie.

4. If you will only show a little patience, that business investment may grow into a(n) _____ for you.

5. The Emancipation Proclamation of 1863 released blacks once and for all from their _____ bonds.

6. They had such a long _____ over the use of the bicycle that their mother finally wouldn't allow either of them to use it.

7. For two nights he did his homework faithfully; then he _____ to his usual lazy ways.

8. When the lights suddenly went out, I _____ my way into the kitchen to find a candle and matches.

1

9. On the ground, teams of paramedics administered first aid to the victims of the accident, while police helicopters _____ overhead.

10. With tireless devotion, the mother kept a(n) _____ at the bedside of her ailing child.

11. What is the exact wording of the _____ about early birds and worm-catching?

12. Suddenly the _____ voices of two people engaged in a quarrel burst upon my ears and jarred me out of my daydream.

13. Your silly pride about doing everything on your own _____ your getting the help you need so badly.

14. Before the new housing project could be built, it was necessary to tear down the old houses and remove the _____ .

15. Our teacher gave Martha and me permission to _____ on our reports since we were investigating related problems.

16. During his 11 years of "personal rule," King Charles I of England bypassed Parliament and ruled the country by royal _____ .

17. A word of praise from the coach meant more to me than all the loud but thoughtless _____ of the crowd.

18. June was only trying to help you, and you hurt her feelings when you reacted to her criticism in such a(n) _____ way.

19. After the walls of their city fell to the enemy, the inhabitants withdrew to the _____ and continued the struggle from there.

20. As we discussed the coming vacation, we gradually _____ a plan for a bicycle trip through New England.

Synonyms *From the words for this unit, choose the one that is most nearly **the same** in meaning as each of the following groups of expressions. Write the word on the line given.*

1. to fumble for, cast about for   _____

2. a fort, stronghold, bulwark, bastion   _____

3. applause, cheers, acclaim   _____

4. wreckage, debris   _____

5. to unfold, develop, emerge   _____

6. a slowpoke, straggler; slow, sluggish   _____

7. to hinder, check, stop   _____

8. slavish, groveling, fawning

9. a proclamation, edict; to proclaim

10. to shove, push, bump

11. to return to, relapse

12. to team up, join forces

13. an extract, portion, section

14. grating, shrill; different, divergent

15. a proverb, maxim

16. to squabble, bicker

17. a sudden profit or gain, windfall

18. rude, surly, ill-tempered

19. to float; to linger; to waver, seesaw

20. a period of watchful attention

Antonyms   From the words for this unit, choose the one that is most nearly **opposite** in meaning to each of the following groups of expressions. Write the word on the line given.

1. harmonious, in agreement

2. boos, disapproval, ridicule

3. an early bird; swift, speedy, prompt

4. courteous, civil, well-mannered

5. to help, promote, facilitate

6. to agree, concur, be of one mind

7. masterly, overbearing

8. to work alone

9. to wither, shrivel up, atrophy

10. a sudden and unexpected loss

11. to progress, go forward to

12. a lack of attention or wakefulness

13. to soar

14. to avoid contact with

15. to grasp firmly and without hesitation

1

Choosing the Right Word   *Encircle the **boldface** word that more satisfactorily completes each of the following sentences.*

1. For weeks an anxious world (**reverted, hovered**) between war and peace as diplomats desperately struggled to resolve the crisis.

2. Under the Articles of Confederation, the 13 states (**evolved, wrangled**) so much that the nation seemed to be in danger of breaking up.

3. The "broken-down old furniture" that Mrs. Rhine left to her children turned out to be a (**bonanza, rubble**) of valuable antiques.

4. From the hundreds of newspaper items, the lawyer carefully (**excerpted, collaborated**) three short paragraphs that supported his case.

5. There are times when we all need to be (**jostled, reverted**) away from old, familiar ideas that may no longer be as true as they once seemed.

6. The committee found it impossible to reach any agreement on the matter because the views of its members were so (**churlish, discordant**).

7. A President needs people who will tell him frankly what they really think, rather than just offer (**servile, laggard**) approval of everything he does.

8. I refuse to accept the excuse that the pressures of a new job caused her to (**revert, grope**) to the habit of cigarette smoking.

9. After I had broken curfew for the third time in one week, my angry parents (**decreed, precluded**) that I was "grounded" for the rest of the term.

10. When I fumbled the ball on the 3-yard line, the (**plaudits, excerpts**) of the crowd suddenly turned into jeers and catcalls.

11. Every time Tom quotes an old (**vigil, adage**), he looks as though he has just had a brilliant new idea.

12. The assembly speaker may have been boring, but that was no excuse for the students' (**laggard, churlish**) behavior toward him.

13. As we searched through the (**rubble, vigil**) after the earthquake, it was heartbreaking to find such articles as a teakettle and a child's doll.

14. After the operation, we sat in the hospital lounge, keeping a nightlong (**bonanza, vigil**) until we heard from the doctor.

15. She was quick to approve new programs for our club but (**servile, laggard**) in providing financial support for them.

16. The fact that he was found guilty of a felony many years ago doesn't (**preclude, evolve**) his running for mayor.

17. Dick raised so many objections to attending the dance that it was obvious he was (**groping, precluding**) for an excuse not to go.

18. I have always regarded our colleges and universities as (**citadels, vigils**) of learning and bastions against ignorance and superstition.

19. All those who (**evolved, collaborated**) with the enemy in the hope of gaining special favors will be punished severely.

20. The little club that they set up to talk over community problems (**evolved, excerpted**) over the years into a national political organization.

Unit 2

Note carefully the spelling, pronunciation, and definition of each of the following words. Then write the word in the blank space in the illustrative phrase following.

1. **antics**
('an tiks)

(*pl. n.*) ridiculous and unpredictable behavior or actions

amused by the _____ of the clowns

2. **avowed**
(ə 'vaüd)

(*adj., part.*) declared openly and without shame, acknowledged

an _____ enemy of the plan

3. **banter**
('ban tər)

(*v.*) to exchange playful remarks, tease; (*n.*) talk that is playful and teasing

_____ good-naturedly with friends

4. **bountiful**
('baünt i fəl)

(*adj.*) giving freely, generous; plentiful, given abundantly

enjoyed the _____ gifts of nature

5. **congested**
(kən 'jest id)

(*adj., part.*) overcrowded, filled or occupied to excess

lungs _____ with fluids

6. **detriment**
('det rə mənt)

(*n.*) harm or loss; injury, damage; a disadvantage; a cause of harm, injury, loss, or damage

a _____ to our cause

7. **durable**
('dür ə bəl)

(*adj.*) sturdy, not easily worn out or destroyed; lasting for a long time; (*n., pl.*) consumer goods used repeatedly over a series of years

a very _____ kind of cloth

8. **enterprising**
('ent ər prī ziŋ)

(*adj.*) energetic, willing and able to start something new; showing boldness and imagination

an _____ young person

9. **frugal**
('frü gəl)

(*adj.*) economical, avoiding waste and luxury; scanty, poor, meager

a _____ but nourishing meal

10. **gingerly**
('jin jər lē)

(*adj., adv.*) with extreme care or caution

handled the newborn baby very _____

11. **glut**
(glət)

(*v.*) to provide more than is needed or wanted; to feed or fill to the point of overstuffing; (*n.*) an oversupply

a _____ on the market

12. **incognito**
(in käg 'nē tō)

(*adj., adv.*) in a disguised state, under an assumed name; (*n.*) the state of being disguised or a person in disguise

a celebrity traveling _____

13. **invalidate**
(in 'val ə dāt)

(*v.*) to make valueless, take away all force or effect

took measures to _____ the contract

14. legendary
('lej ən der ē)

(*adj.*) described in well-known stories; existing in old stories (legends) rather than in real life

one of Rome's _____ heroes

15. maim
(mām)

(*v.*) to cripple, disable

a fall that could _____ him for life

16. minimize
('min ə mīz)

(*v.*) to make as small as possible, make the least of; to make smaller than before

take measures to _____ the risk

17. oblique
(ō 'blēk)

(*adj.*) slanting or sloping; not straightforward or direct

an _____ blow that did little damage

18. veer
(vēr)

(*v.*) to change direction or course, turn aside, shift

_____ from one side to the other

19. venerate
('ven ə rāt)

(*v.*) to regard with reverence, look up to with great respect

taught to _____ their leaders

20. wanton
('wänt ən)

(*adj.*) reckless; heartless, unjustifiable; loose in morals; (*n.*) a spoiled, pampered person; one with low morals

guilty of _____ cruelty

Completing the Sentence

From the words for this unit, choose the one that best completes each of the following sentences. Write the word in the space provided.

1. Since I was afraid of banging my bare feet against the furniture, I walked through the darkened room very _____ .

2. We admired the _____ immigrant who set up a small shop and developed it into a large and prosperous business.

3. Isn't it strange for a(n) _____ music lover to show no interest in our school orchestra?

4. The vandals broke windows, overturned desks, and left the school a scene of _____ destruction.

5. Instead of walking straight from the farmhouse to the road, we set off in a(n) _____ direction across the field.

6. Although he had been severely _____ in the automobile accident, he was determined to return to his job and lead a normal life.

7. What a change from the _____ streets of the inner city to the wide-open spaces of the Great Plains!

8. As Americans, we _____ the great ideals of human freedom expressed in the Bill of Rights.

9. I would never have expected members of the senior class to take part in such childish _____ !

10. The film star traveled _____ in order to avoid the attentions of his adoring fans.

11. To avoid the children in the street, the truck _____ sharply to the right and sideswiped several parked cars.

12. Although she tried to cover it up with lively _____ , I could see that her feelings had been deeply hurt.

13. Even the most _____ materials will in time be worn away by flowing water.

14. While I do not wish to alarm you, I will not _____ the danger if you refuse to have the children vaccinated.

15. Davy Crockett was a real person, but so many tall stories have been told about him that he has become a(n) _____ figure.

16. We should be willing to share our _____ food supplies with less fortunate people in other parts of the world.

17. Although his income was small, his _____ living habits enabled him to save a large sum of money over the years.

18. In American law, the fact that the person accused of a crime is poor does not _____ his or her right to adequate legal representation.

19. When we desperately needed every bit of help we could find, what we got was a(n) _____ of advice and a scarcity of cold cash.

20. Inability to get along smoothly and effectively with other people will be a great _____ to you in any career you may choose.

Synonyms   *From the words for this unit, choose the one that is most nearly **the same** in meaning as each of the following groups of expressions. Write the word on the line given.*

1. rash; malicious, spiteful; unprovoked   _____

2. to injure, cripple; to mar, disfigure, mutilate   _____

3. to worship, revere, idolize   _____

4. in disguise, under an assumed identity   _____

5. injury, harm; a hindrance, liability   _____

6. cautiously, warily, circumspectly   _____

7. to belittle, downplay, underrate   _____

8. to cancel, annul; to disprove, discredit   _____

9. liberal, abundant, copious   _____

10. slanted, diagonal; indirect _____

11. jammed, packed, choked _____

12. to swerve, change course suddenly _____

13. admitted, declared; sworn _____

14. thrifty; meager, skimpy _____

15. vigorous, ambitious, aggressive, audacious _____

16. to flood, inundate; a surplus, plethora _____

17. pranks, shenanigans _____

18. sturdy, long-lasting, enduring _____

19. teasing, joking, raillery _____

20. mythical, fabulous; famous, celebrated _____

Antonyms   *From the words for this unit, choose the one that is most nearly **opposite** in meaning to each of the following groups of expressions. Write the word on the line given.*

1. a shortage, scarcity, dearth, paucity _____

2. to support, confirm, back up; to legalize _____

3. wasteful, improvident; lavish, extravagant _____

4. uncluttered, unimpeded _____

5. to magnify, enlarge, exaggerate _____

6. fragile, perishable; fleeting, ephemeral _____

7. firmly, confidently, aggressively _____

8. direct, straight to the point _____

9. scarce, scanty, in short supply _____

10. an advantage, help, plus _____

11. lazy, indolent; timid, diffident _____

12. a serious talk or discussion _____

13. to move ahead in a straight line _____

14. unacknowledged, undisclosed _____

15. to despise, detest; to ridicule, deride _____

16. undisguised _____

17. justified; morally strict; responsible _____

Choosing the Right Word

*Encircle the **boldface** word that more satisfactorily completes each of the following sentences.*

1. Self-confidence is a good quality, but if it is carried too far, it can be a (**detriment, glut**) to success in life.

2. We were shocked by their (**bountiful, wanton**) misuse of the money their parents had left them.

3. As an (**avowed, legendary**) supporter of women's rights, she believes that men and women should receive the same pay if they do the same jobs.

4. Instead of just waiting for things to "get better" by themselves, we must be more (**frugal, enterprising**) in working for improvements.

5. Sally's speech would have been better if she had stayed with her main idea instead of (**bantering, veering**) off to side issues.

6. Why do you suppose someone whose face is known all over the world would want to travel (**obliquely, incognito**)?

7. Instead of approaching him in that timid and (**frugal, gingerly**) manner, tell him frankly what is on your mind.

8. Building a new skyscraper there will only bring additional thousands of people into an area that is already (**invalidated, congested**).

9. I didn't want Charlotte to know that I was watching her, but occasionally I managed to steal a few (**oblique, legendary**) glances at her.

10. Children may be (**maimed, avowed**) in spirit as well as in body if they do not have a secure and loving home environment.

11. When they saw that they had been caught red-handed, they resorted to all kinds of (**gluts, antics**) in a vain attempt to prove their "innocence."

12. We are grateful for the (**frugal, bountiful**) gifts that our great artists and composers have given us.

13. The (**legendary, wanton**) deeds of Sherlock Holmes are so well known that many people think he really lived.

14. It was bad taste on Mark's part to use that (**venerating, bantering**) tone when we were discussing such a sad event.

15. After living for so long on a (**frugal, bountiful**) diet, I was amazed when I saw the variety of rich dishes served at the banquet.

16. Although I love sports, I sometimes feel that television is becoming (**glutted, invalidated**) with athletic events of all kinds.

17. Because of Bob's repeated traffic violations, his driver's license has been (**congested, invalidated**).

18. Our friendship has proved to be (**durable, enterprising**) because it is based on mutual respect and honesty.

19. I will not try to (**minimize, banter**) the difficulties we face, but I am sure that we can overcome them by working together.

20. The mad Roman emperor Caligula believed that he was a god and expected people to (**venerate, minimize**) him as such.

Unit 3

Definitions   *Note carefully the spelling, pronunciation, and definition of each of the following words. Then write the word in the blank space in the illustrative phrase following.*

1. allot
(ə 'lät)

(*v.*) to assign or distribute into shares or portions

_____ us the necessary funds

2. amass
(ə 'mas)

(*v.*) to bring together, collect, gather, especially for oneself; to come together, assemble

_____ a fortune in the stock market

3. audacious
(ô 'dā shəs)

(*adj.*) bold, adventurous, recklessly daring

_____ feats of the trapeze artists

4. comply
(kəm 'plī)

(*v.*) to yield to a request or command

willing to _____ with your wishes

5. devoid
(di 'void)

(*adj.*) not having or using, lacking

a well _____ of water

6. elite
(ā 'lēt)

(*n.*) the choice part of a group of people or things; (*adj.*) superior

the social _____ of the community

7. grapple
('grap əl)

(*n.*) an iron hook used to grab and hold; (*v.*) to come to grips with, wrestle with, fight with

_____ with the thief

8. incapacitate
(in kə 'pas ə tāt)

(*v.*) to deprive of strength or ability; to make legally ineligible

_____ by old age

9. instigate
('in stə gāt)

(*v.*) to urge on; to stir up

did their best to _____ a riot

10. longevity
(län 'jev ə tē)

(*n.*) long life, long duration

the _____ of the sea turtle

11. myriad
('mir ē əd)

(*adj.*) in very great numbers; (*n.*) a very great number

the _____ life-forms of the jungle

12. perspective
(pər 'spek tiv)

(*n.*) a point of view or general standpoint from which different things are viewed, physically or mentally; the appearance to the eye of various objects at a given time, place, or distance

drawn to scale and in the right _____

13. perturb
(pər 'tərb)

(*v.*) to trouble, make uneasy; to disturb greatly; to throw into confusion

_____ by their rude behavior

14. prodigious
(prə ′dij əs)

(*adj.*) immense, extraordinary in bulk, size, or degree

the _____ mind of Albert Einstein

15. relevant
(′rel ə vənt)

(*adj.*) connected with or related to the matter at hand

provided the _____ information

16. skittish
(′skit ish)

(*adj.*) extremely nervous and easily frightened; shy or timid; extremely cautious; unstable, undependable

a _____ horse

17. tether
(′teth er)

(*n.*) a rope or chain used to fasten something to a fixed object; the outer limit of strength or resources; (*v.*) to fasten with a rope or chain

_____ the boat to the dock

18. unison
(′yü nə sən)

(*n.*) a sounding together; agreement or accord

choirs singing in _____

19. vie
(vī)

(*v.*) to compete; to strive for victory or superiority

_____ for top honors in physics

20. willful
(′wil fəl)

(*adj.*) stubbornly self-willed; done on purpose, deliberate

found guilty of _____ murder

Completing the Sentence

From the words for this unit, choose the one that best completes each of the following sentences. Write the word in the space provided.

1. The _____ child insisted on wearing sneakers to her sister's wedding.

2. Trying to navigate through rush-hour traffic on a high-speed expressway can be a nightmare for a(n) _____ driver.

3. You will have to use a(n) _____ to recover the lobster trap from the bottom of the bay.

4. He joined the _____ group of athletes who have run a mile in under four minutes.

5. A number of cities _____ with one another to be chosen as the site of the national political convention.

6. Since the town meeting tonight has been called to deal with conservation, only discussion _____ to that subject will be allowed.

7. Before setting out on the camping trip, Mr. Silver _____ special tasks and responsibilities to all of us.

8. I am completely _____ of sympathy for anyone who loses a job because of carelessness and indifference.

9. The disease had so _____ the poor woman that she was no longer able to leave her bed.

10. The autumn night sky, with its _____ of stars, always fills me with awe and wonder.

11. There in the middle of the garden was a goat _____ to a stake.

12. Even though Ellen is a brilliant student, I don't quite understand how she could _____ such a vast store of information so quickly.

13. If all the members of the cast work in _____ , I am sure we will have a successful class show.

14. When he seemed hopelessly defeated, Washington crossed the Delaware and launched a(n) _____ surprise attack on the Hessians.

15. Some of our best secret agents were sent behind enemy lines in an effort to _____ a rebellion.

16. Father said, "I am _____ not because you failed the exam but because you still seem unable to understand _why_ you failed it."

17. Though we have made many outstanding contributions to the conquest of space, landing men on the moon is probably our most _____ achievement.

18. Someday, when you see this event in its proper _____ , you will realize that it is not as important as it seems now.

19. We can thank modern medical science for the increased _____ of human beings in most parts of the world.

20. I refuse to _____ with any order issued by a person who has absolutely no knowledge of the project I'm working on.

Synonyms   _From the words for this unit, choose the one that is most nearly **the same** in meaning as each of the following groups of expressions. Write the word on the line given._

1. gigantic, tremendous; astounding   _____

2. harmonious agreement or accord   _____

3. headstrong, obstinate; premeditated   _____

4. countless, innumerable   _____

5. to tie up, chain up, leash   _____

6. to provoke, start, incite   _____

7. to compete, contend, be rivals   _____

8. length of life   _____

9. jumpy, nervous, restive; timid; capricious, fickle _____

10. to submit to, consent to, acquiesce in _____

11. having a direct bearing on, pertinent _____

12. to disable, debilitate, paralyze, cripple _____

13. bold, daring, enterprising _____

14. to parcel out, apportion, assign _____

15. the cream of the crop; the upper crust _____

16. lacking, wanting, bereft _____

17. to upset, agitate; to anger, irritate _____

18. to tackle, confront, struggle with _____

19. to accumulate, pile up; to garner _____

20. a sense of proportion, a way of looking at things _____

Antonyms   *From the words for this unit, choose the one that is most nearly **opposite** in meaning to each of the following groups of expressions. Write the word on the line given.*

1. obedient, docile, tractable _____

2. beside the point, unconnected, extraneous _____

3. to reject, refuse, decline _____

4. few in number, scanty, sparse _____

5. full, teeming, abounding _____

6. timid, cowardly _____

7. to delight, gladden, please _____

8. to untie, let loose _____

9. puny, minuscule; insignificant _____

10. the rank and file; the dregs of society _____

11. to stop, quell, squelch, quash _____

12. bold, daring, reckless; cool, unflappable _____

13. to scatter, dissipate; to squander, waste _____

14. to rehabilitate, make whole again _____

15. brevity of duration, transience _____

3

Choosing the Right Word   *Encircle the **boldface** word that more satisfactorily completes each of the following sentences.*

1. I don't think anyone can hope to (**vie, comply**) with Gloria in the election for "Most Popular Student."

2. After listening to their nasty gossip for several hours, I reached the end of my (**perspective, tether**) and lost my temper.

3. The bitter strike closed shops, shut down factories, and (**incapacitated, instigated**) an entire industry for months.

4. We will never have a well-organized or effective club if all the members insist (**willfully, prodigiously**) on having their own way.

5. As I stared at the luscious chocolate swirl cake, I bravely (**complied, grappled**) with temptation — but the chocolate cake won!

6. He has had such bad experiences with motorcycles that he has become extremely (**audacious, skittish**) of them.

7. He delivered a simple, low-key speech, completely (**devoid, relevant**) of fancy language or emotional appeals.

8. Our course in life science has given us some idea of the (**myriad, unison**) varieties of plants and animals inhabiting the earth.

9. How do you explain the fact that in practically every country the (**elite, longevity**) of women is greater than that of men?

10. People who come from rich and socially prominent families don't always belong to the intellectual (**myriad, elite**).

11. Jane Addams was not only profoundly (**perturbed, instigated**) by the sufferings of other people but tried hard to help them.

12. In the next chorus, *please* try to sing in (**unison, compliance**).

13. If we have to share the same locker, please try to keep your things in the space (**allotted, amassed**) to you.

14. Perhaps in the long-term (**longevity, perspective**) of history, some events that seem very important now will prove to be minor.

15. The defense has told you about the defendant's unhappy childhood, but how is this (**relevant, willful**) to the question of innocence or guilt?

16. Unless you want to (**instigate, amass**) a quarrel, don't tell Ray that you saw me at the rink with another boy.

17. Can you imagine what a (**relevant, prodigious**) amount of research is needed for a multivolume reference book like the *Encyclopaedia Britannica*?

18. She had devoted her life to (**amassing, allotting**) not material riches but the love, respect, and thanks of every member of this community.

19. I wonder why the camp directors were unwilling to (**comply, vie**) with my request to keep a pet snake in my tent.

20. Great new discoveries in science can be made only by men and women with intellectual (**compliance, audacity**).

Review   Units 1–3

Analogies   *In each of the following, encircle the item that best completes the comparison.*

1. frugal is to **bountiful** as
a. oblique is to slanting
b. timid is to audacious
c. churlish is to expensive
d. willful is to graceful

2. wanton is to **unfavorable** as
a. servile is to favorable
b. durable is to unfavorable
c. enterprising is to favorable
d. gingerly is to unfavorable

3. daredevil is to **audacious** as
a. spendthrift is to frugal
b. laggard is to enterprising
c. tattletale is to prodigious
d. coward is to skittish

4. amass is to **much** as
a. minimize is to little
b. reduce is to much
c. increase is to little
d. shrink is to much

5. boor is to **churlish** as
a. traitor is to faithful
b. angle is to oblique
c. lion is to skittish
d. toady is to servile

6. veer is to **away** as
a. inflate is to down
b. revert is to back
c. wither is to up
d. decline is to forward

7. scarce is to **devoid** as
a. bountiful is to glutted
b. legendary is to relevant
c. unison is to discordant
d. servile is to decreed

8. lungs are to **congested** as
a. streets are to deserted
b. citadels are to strong
c. vigils are to nightly
d. drains are to clogged

9. wrangle is to **discordant** as
a. agree is to harmonious
b. grope is to certain
c. comply is to willful
d. perturb is to pleasant

10. agitator is to **instigate** as
a. saint is to venerate
b. laggard is to hurry
c. spark is to ignite
d. perspective is to evolve

11. gingerly is to **care** as
a. laggard is to speed
b. diplomatic is to tact
c. skittish is to courage
d. churlish is to courtesy

12. words are to **banter** as
a. pictures are to adages
b. actions are to antics
c. ideas are to bonanzas
d. deeds are to plaudits

13. myriad is to **many** as
a. devoid is to none
b. scarce is to much
c. glutted is to little
d. congested is to few

14. tether is to **rope** as
a. hover is to bird
b. maim is to detriment
c. grapple is to hook
d. minimize is to tool

15. avowed is to **openness** as
a. frank is to concealment
b. stealthy is to openness
c. incognito is to concealment
d. underhanded is to openness

16. durable is to **longevity** as
a. relevant is to great wealth
b. unified is to great variety
c. elite is to great wisdom
d. prodigious is to great size

17. audacious is to **plaudits** as
a. legendary is to heroes
b. prodigious is to strength
c. clownish is to antics
d. cowardly is to jeers

18. miser is to **amass** as
a. spendthrift is to squander
b. thief is to inherit
c. banker is to embezzle
d. wanton is to save

R

Identification *In each of the following groups, encircle the word that is best defined or suggested by the introductory phrase.*

1. an order having the force of law
a. grapple   b. wrangle   c. decree   d. rubble

2. "All together, now. One, two, three!"
a. gropingly   b. unison   c. skittishly   d. willfully

3. a highly profitable investment
a. wanton   b. bonanza   c. tether   d. citadel

4. with no concern for right or justice
a. wanton   b. laggard   c. servile   d. legendary

5. a small group of the best students chosen for a special course
a. vigil   b. elite   c. rubble   d. bonanza

6. scattered paragraphs from the Constitution
a. plaudits   b. decrees   c. excerpts   d. gluts

7. so many troubles that I can't begin to count them
a. discordant   b. devoid   c. churlish   d. myriad

8. a horse that "spooks easily"
a. audacious   b. willful   c. skittish   d. laggard

9. a book written by several people
a. congestion   b. collaboration   c. compliance   d. incapacitation

10. a ray of light hitting the window at an angle
a. relevant   b. oblique   c. avowed   d. wanton

11. to keep going back to one's old habits
a. revert   b. vie   c. instigate   d. minimize

12. more goods on the market than can be sold
a. perspective   b. longevity   c. glut   d. adage

13. to assign storage space to all the tenants
a. invalidate   b. allot   c. evolve   d. amass

14. a parched and arid wasteland
a. myriad   b. devoid   c. avowed   d. incognito

15. what remains when a city has been heavily bombed
a. amass   b. detriment   c. rubble   d. maim

16. a person who admits something openly
a. avowed   b. bountiful   c. frugal   d. durable

17. to take steps to prevent something from happening
a. jostle   b. preclude   c. veer   d. hover

18. cheers and applause at the end of a performance
a. antics   b. grapples   c. banter   d. plaudits

19. a worker who has lost a finger in an industrial accident
a. prodigious   b. gingerly   c. churlish   d. maimed

20. to cause worry and grief to parents by one's conduct
a. venerate   b. perturb   c. preclude   d. evolve

Shades of   *Read each sentence carefully. Then encircle the item*
Meaning   *that best completes the statement below the sentence.*

By a famous Constitutional compromise the "official" population of the pre-
Civil War Southern states was determined by adding three-fifths of the   (2)
servile population to the total free population.

1. In line 3 the word **servile** most nearly means
   a. enslaved   b. fawning   c. submissive   d. domestic

Thereupon ensued the laughable spectacle of the old king's courtiers
jostling with upstarts for places in the new king's retinue.   (2)

2. The word **jostling** in line 2 is best defined as
   a. bumping   b. debating   c. shoving   d. vying

"It's amazing that they can work such long hours under such difficult
conditions with no apparent detriment to their health," she observed.   (2)

3. The phrase **detriment to** in line 2 is used to mean
   a. change in   c. improvement in
   b. damage to   d. source of harm to

One of the indicators by which experts measure the state of the economy
tracks national sales of cars, refrigerators, and other durables.   (2)

4. In line 2 the word **durables** most nearly means
   a. heavy equipment   c. grains and cereals
   b. technological gadgetry   d. substantial consumer goods

Serious fighting broke out well before the bulk of either of the opposing
armies had amassed on the battlefield.   (2)

5. The best meaning for **amassed** in line 2 is
   a. brought together   c. assembled
   b. hoarded   d. garnered

Antonyms   *In each of the following groups, encircle the word that is*
*most nearly the **opposite** of the first word in **boldface***
***type**.*

1. audacious	**3. incapacitate**	**5. discordant**	**7. gingerly**
a. tired	a. kindle	a. jarring	a. quickly
b. timid	b. adjust	b. heartfelt	b. boldly
c. hard	c. rehabilitate	c. harmonious	c. sadly
d. lasting	d. disfigure	d. playful	d. slowly
2. amass	**4. preclude**	**6. venerate**	**8. laggard**
a. fill	a. give back	a. proclaim	a. untimely
b. take	b. take out	b. revere	b. early
c. squander	c. make shorter	c. hunt	c. punctured
d. return	d. make possible	d. despise	d. behindhand

9. durable
a. easy
b. nice
c. fragile
d. dangerous

10. relevant
a. unrelated
b. false
c. good
d. pleasant

11. oblique
a. early
b. careful
c. direct
d. simple

12. minimize
a. prevent
b. smother
c. insist
d. exaggerate

13. comply
a. refuse
b. struggle
c. receive
d. annoy

14. avowed
a. few
b. secret
c. sad
d. careful

15. bountiful
a. cautious
b. stingy
c. large
d. tough

16. instigate
a. blame
b. return
c. ignore
d. stop

17. incognito
a. smartly
b. simply
c. openly
d. directly

18. congested
a. deserted
b. allowed
c. helped
d. related

19. willful
a. stingy
b. selfish
c. solid
d. obedient

20. churlish
a. straight
b. small
c. polite
d. poor

Completing the Sentence

From the following words, choose the one that best completes each of the sentences below. Write the word in the appropriate space.

Group A

adage	myriad	grope	plaudits
venerate	decree	rubble	legendary
detriment	perspective	bonanza	jostle

1. As people grow older and more experienced, they are usually able to see failures and disappointments in a better _____ .
2. It was so dark during our overnight hike that we had to _____ our way through the forest.
3. We have all heard of the _____ monster that is supposed to live in Loch Ness, Scotland.
4. If there is any truth in the old _____ that "birds of a feather flock together," then you and I should be close friends.
5. "Not in the clamor of the crowded street, Not in the shouts and _____ of the throng, But in ourselves, are triumph and defeat." (Longfellow)

Group B

minimize	hover	invalidate	citadel
vigil	tether	collaborate	prodigious
banter	allot	wanton	elite

1. For days after the fire, smoke _____ over the burned-out buildings, and a foul stench permeated the air.

2. The grief-stricken soldiers kept a nightlong _____ beside the body of their fallen leader.

3. You cannot be successful on this test unless you _____ a reasonable amount of time to each question.

4. Throughout the long campaign, her _____ energy enabled her to keep going when everyone else was on the verge of exhaustion.

5. We could tell from the happy _____ in one locker room and the glum silence in the other which was the winning team.

Word Families

A. *On the line provided, write a **noun form** of each of the following words.*

EXAMPLE: willful — **willfulness**

1. frugal _____

2. venerate _____

3. audacious _____

4. collaborate _____

5. comply _____

6. allot _____

7. enterprising _____

8. instigate _____

9. evolve _____

10. invalidate _____

B. *On the line provided, write a **verb form** of each of the following words.*

EXAMPLE: invalidation — **invalidate**

1. durable _____

2. evolution _____

3. incapacitation _____

4. plaudits _____

5. instigation _____

6. avowed _____

7. minimally _____

8. reversion _____

9. congestion _____

10. veneration _____

**Filling
the Blanks**

*Encircle the pair of words that best complete the
meaning of each of the following sets of sentences.*

1. "A person has to expect a little accidental bumping and pushing in a
crowded bus," I observed to my companion. "It's just not possible to
avoid _____ another passenger when the center aisle is
_____ with people."
   a. maiming . . . devoid
   b. grappling . . . elite
   c. minimizing . . . glutted
   d. jostling . . . congested

2. It isn't wise to give very young children toys that will break easily. They
need playthings that are _____ because they haven't yet
learned to handle fragile items _____ .
   a. servile . . . churlishly
   b. durable . . . gingerly
   c. frugal . . . willfully
   d. prodigious . . . wantonly

3. If you are careless with your money, you will always be penniless, but if
you are _____ , you may be able to _____
a sizable personal fortune.
   a. bountiful . . . evolve
   b. enterprising . . . maim
   c. frugal . . . amass
   d. audacious . . . preclude

4. A man of prodigious energy and _____ , he rose in no time
at all from relatively humble beginnings to the very _____ of
power.
   a. enterprise . . . citadels
   b. compliance . . . perspectives
   c. longevity . . . antics
   d. audacity . . . durables

5. "If he weren't so rude, I'd be glad to _____ with him on the
project," I said. "But I don't think I can work with someone who always
behaves in such a _____ manner."
   a. wrangle . . . servile
   b. collaborate . . . churlish
   c. banter . . . relevant
   d. vie . . . unison

6. The clownish _____ of such Disney characters as Donald
Duck and Goofy have won the hearts and _____ of many
generations of delighted children.
   a. banter . . . bonanzas
   b. antics . . . plaudits
   c. adages . . . vigils
   d. tethers . . . decrees

7. The TV marathon not only garnered _____ amounts of
money for Africa's starving millions but also yielded an unexpectedly
rich _____ of publicity for their plight.
   a. myriad . . . rubble
   b. legendary . . . allotment
   c. prodigious . . . bonanza
   d. bountiful . . . banter

Unit 4

Note carefully the spelling, pronunciation, and definition of each of the following words. Then write the word in the blank space in the illustrative phrase following.

1. annul
(ə 'nəl)

(v.) to reduce to nothing; to make ineffective or inoperative; to declare legally invalid or void

wish to _____ the out-of-date law

2. blasé
(blä 'zā)

(adj.) indifferent, bored as a result of having enjoyed many pleasures

a very _____ attitude

3. bolster
('bōl stər)

(v.) to support, give a boost to; (n.) a long pillow or cushion; a supporting post

offer facts to _____ his argument

4. deplore
(di 'plôr)

(v.) to feel or express regret or disapproval

_____ his lack of good manners

5. frivolous
('friv ə ləs)

(adj.) of little importance, not worthy of serious attention; not meant seriously

a _____ suggestion

6. muster
('məs tər)

(v.) to bring together for service or battle; to gather or summon; to amount to, comprise, include; (n.) a list of men for military service; a gathering, accumulation

_____ up courage to face the bully

7. nonentity
(nän 'en tə tē)

(n.) a person or thing of no importance

refuse to be treated as a _____

8. obsess
(äb 'ses)

(v.) to trouble, haunt, or fill the mind

is _____ with a fear of failure

9. ornate
(ôr 'nāt)

(adj.) elaborately decorated; showily splendid

too _____ a frame for so simple a picture

10. oust
(aùst)

(v.) to remove, drive out of a position or place

_____ from office by the military

11. peruse
(pə 'rüz)

(v.) to read thoroughly and carefully

have a lawyer _____ the agreement

12. porous
('pôr əs)

(adj.) full of tiny holes; able to be penetrated by air or water

as _____ as a sponge

13. promontory
('präm ən tôr ē)

(n.) a high point of land extending into water

high on a _____ overlooking the sea

14. prone
(prōn)

(*adj.*) lying face down; inclined, likely

unfortunately _____ to giggling

15. qualm
(kwäm)

(*n.*) a pang of conscience, uneasiness, misgiving, or doubt; a feeling of faintness or nausea

have _____ about criticizing him

16. recourse
('rē kôrs)

(*n.*) a person or thing turned to for help or advice; the act of seeking help or protection

have _____ to a higher authority

17. residue
('rez ə dü)

(*n.*) a remainder, that which remains when a part has been used up or removed

left a sticky _____ in the pan

18. solicitous
(sə 'lis ət əs)

(*adj.*) showing concern or care; fearful or anxious about someone or something

a _____ inquiry about her health

19. staid
(stād)

(*adj.*) serious and dignified; quiet or subdued in character or conduct

dressed in _____ greys and browns

20. sustain
(sə 'stān)

(*v.*) to support, nourish, keep up; to suffer, undergo; to bear up under, withstand; to affirm the validity of

_____ a serious injury

Completing the Sentence

From the words for this unit, choose the one that best completes each of the following sentences. Write the word in the space provided.

1. When we heard about Walt's serious illness, we visited him daily in the hospital to _____ his low morale.

2. The two sisters are very different — one lively and fun loving, the other quiet and rather _____ .

3. Certain saltlike chemicals may effectively prevent the streets from icing up in winter, but the powdery _____ they leave behind can damage footwear.

4. You should _____ the instructions with great care before you fill out your application for admission.

5. "In that barren wasteland," the explorer said, "we had great difficulty finding enough food to _____ life."

6. He seems to have no _____ about being unfair to other people to gain his own ends.

7. His public statements became so embarrassing that club members tried to _____ him from the presidency.

8. When Dan returned home after his first year in college, he tried to impress us with his sophisticated and _____ manner.

9. Ms. Bauer is the kind of _____ teacher who aids and encourages her students in every way she can.

10. A lighthouse was built on the tip of the _____ , where it served as a beacon for ships many miles away.

11. I will not allow a single act of carelessness to _____ the results of years of hard work.

12. The furnishings in their house are so _____ that the place looks more like a museum than a family home.

13. If you feel that you have been cheated, your only _____ is to make a complaint to the Consumer Bureau in your city.

14. It is now time for you to take your work seriously and to give up some of the _____ activities of your earlier years.

15. I do not criticize people for trying to get ahead, but I _____ any attempt to take unfair advantage of others.

16. There I was—an utter _____ in a group of famous and accomplished persons!

17. When we tried to carry water from the well, we found to our dismay that the bottom of the old bucket was _____ .

18. Every able-bodied man will be _____ into active military service to fight off the invading force.

19. Because the villagers have so few dealings with the outside world, they are _____ to regard strangers with deep distrust.

20. Every girl wants to look her best, but Judy carries this to the point where she seems to be _____ with her appearance.

Synonyms *From the words for this unit, choose the one that is most nearly **the same** in meaning as each of the following groups of expressions. Write the word on the line given.*

1. concerned, anxious _____

2. to assemble, mobilize, marshal; roster, inventory _____

3. lying face down, prostrate; liable, apt _____

4. to expel, eject _____

5. silly, foolish, inane; petty, trifling _____

6. something a person can turn to for help _____

7. to strengthen, reinforce, buttress; to validate _____

8. fancy, elaborate, flashy, flamboyant _____

9. sedate, sober, prim _____

10. a remnant; the remains, leavings _____

11. bored, indifferent, apathetic _____

12. a nobody _____

13. to nourish, foster; to maintain; to undergo _____

14. a cliff, headland _____

15. to cancel, abolish, invalidate, nullify _____

16. to preoccupy, monopolize one's mind _____

17. leaky, permeable _____

18. to lament, bemoan, bewail _____

19. a regret, second thought, scruple _____

20. to study, pore over, scrutinize _____

Antonyms *From the words for this unit, choose the one that is most nearly **opposite** in meaning to each of the following groups of expressions. Write the word on the line given.*

1. to admit, welcome _____

2. simple, plain, stark, austere _____

3. gaudy, jaunty; unconventional _____

4. to approve; to commend, extol _____

5. enthusiastic, passionate, fervent _____

6. standing upright; unlikely _____

7. airtight and waterproof, impermeable _____

8. to disband, dismiss, disperse _____

9. unconcerned, indifferent, apathetic _____

10. to validate, authorize, ratify _____

11. a celebrity, superstar _____

12. to undermine, weaken, impair _____

13. serious; important, significant _____

14. to glance quickly at, scan _____

Choosing the Right Word   *Encircle the **boldface** word that more satisfactorily completes each of the following sentences.*

1. I admire the way Anne delivered a long, involved speech entirely without (**muster, recourse**) to written notes.

2. If you want to learn to play chess, I suggest that you begin by (**bolstering, perusing**) a summary of the rules.

3. When the mile run began, Ken quickly took the lead, but we knew that he could not (**sustain, obsess**) that pace for the entire race.

4. We learned that behind the old professor's (**ornate, staid**) exterior there was a keen wit and a lively sense of what life is all about.

5. Because they failed to deliver the goods on time, we feel justified in (**annulling, perusing**) the entire contract.

6. The way he blushed and stuttered when questioned (**bolstered, ousted**) my suspicions that he was not telling the truth.

7. The wonderful woman could not have been more (**solicitous, porous**) about me if she had been my own mother.

8. Roy tried to appear (**obsessed, blasé**) when he was named to the Honor Society, but I know that he was thrilled by it.

9. He has a very (**staid, ornate**) writing style, using many unusual words, figures of speech, and involved constructions.

10. The team doctor ran onto the field toward the (**prone, solicitous**) figure of the injured football player.

11. After the claims of all the creditors have been satisfied, the (**residue, recourse**) of the estate will be shared by the children.

12. Only a person who is (**obsessed, bolstered**) with a desire to create beautiful music can become a great pianist or violinist.

13. It is all very well to criticize and (**bolster, deplore**) the mistakes of young people, but why don't you give them credit for their good qualities?

14. I hope some day to build a house on that (**promontory, nonentity**) commanding a beautiful view of the bay.

15. Isn't it strange that such great writers as Poe and Dickinson were considered (**nonentities, promontories**) in their own lifetimes?

16. While her memory is as retentive as a steel trap, mine seems to be as (**porous, blasé**) as a sieve.

17. I like jokes as much as anyone, but I don't approve of making such (**frivolous, porous**) remarks when a serious matter is under discussion.

18. I believed at the time that I was justified in refusing to help her, but later I felt some (**qualms, recourse**) about it.

19. After being the apple of her eye for years, I suddenly found myself (**ousted, bolstered**) from her affections by an upstart rival.

20. "It will take all the strength we can (**annul, muster**) to dislodge the enemy from that hill," the general observed grimly.

Definitions

Note carefully the spelling, pronunciation, and definition of each of the following words. Then write the word in the blank space in the illustrative phrase following.

1. aghast
(ə ′gast)

(*adj.*) filled with amazement, disgust, fear, or terror

_____ at the brutality of the crime

2. ample
(′am pəl)

(*adj.*) more than enough, large, spacious

enjoying an _____ food supply

3. apparition
(ap ə ′rish ən)

(*n.*) a ghost or ghostly figure; an unexplained or unusual appearance

startled by the _____

4. assert
(ə ′sərt)

(*v.*) to declare or state as truth, maintain or defend, put forward forcefully

_____ that he was not guilty

5. cower
(′kaủ ər)

(*v.*) to crouch or shrink away from in fear or shame

_____ in the corner

6. disdain
(dis ′dān)

(*v.*) to look upon with scorn; to refuse scornfully; (*n.*) a feeling of contempt

have only _____ for racists

7. epitaph
(′ep ə taf)

(*n.*) a brief statement written on a tomb or gravestone

write his own_____

8. ethical
(′eth ə kəl)

(*adj.*) having to do with morals, values, right and wrong; in accordance with standards of right conduct; requiring a prescription for purchase

raised important _____ questions

9. facetious
(fə ′sē shəs)

(*adj.*) humorous, not meant seriously

laughing at her _____ remarks

10. inaudible
(in ′ô də bəl)

(*adj.*) not able to be heard

_____ to the human ear

11. indiscriminate
(in dis ′krim ə nət)

(*adj.*) without restraint or control; unselective

_____ slaughter during the raid

12. intrigue
(*n.*, ′in trēg;
v., in ′trēg)

(*n.*) crafty dealings, underhanded plotting; (*v.*) to form and carry out plots; to puzzle or excite the curiosity

uncover a network of _____

13. jurisdiction
(jür is ′dik shən)

(*n.*) an area of authority or control; the right to administer justice

comes under the _____ of the state

14. plausible
(′plô zə bəl)

(*adj.*) appearing true, reasonable, or fair

an excuse that does not seem _____

15. plebeian
(plə 'bē ən)

(*adj.*) common, vulgar; belonging to the lower class; (*n.*) a common person, member of the lower class

_____ tastes

16. prodigal
('präd ə gəl)

(*adj.*) wastefully extravagant; lavishly or generously abundant; (*n.*) one who is wasteful and self-indulgent

_____ with gifts at Christmastime

17. proximity
(präk 'sim ə tē)

(*n.*) nearness, closeness

the _____ of the two homes

18. pulverize
('pəl və rīz)

(*v.*) to grind or pound to a powder or dust; to destroy or overcome (as though by smashing into fragments)

a mill to _____ grain

19. sequel
('sē kwəl)

(*n.*) that which follows, a result; a literary work or film continuing the story of one made earlier

wrote a _____ to his best-seller

20. volatile
('väl ə təl)

(*adj.*) highly changeable, fickle; tending to become violent or explosive; changing readily from the liquid to the gaseous state

puzzled by her _____ behavior

Completing the Sentence

From the words for this unit, choose the one that best completes each of the following sentences. Write the word in the space provided.

1. The writer of the mystery story set up an interesting situation, but in my opinion the ending was not _____ .

2. The way the child _____ in fear whenever an adult spoke to him gave me the impression that he had been mistreated from infancy.

3. With quiet dignity, Mrs. Pollack _____ to answer the insulting question.

4. A(n) _____ TV viewer, who watches any programs, good or bad, is bound to waste a lot of time.

5. The giant crushers lifted the boulders and quickly _____ them into a uniform gray powder.

6. For the moment the crowd was quiet and subdued, but we knew that it was so _____ that it might become ugly and dangerous at any time.

7. Observers on the ground were _____ to see the plane suddenly burst into flames and plunge headlong into the harbor.

8. Did Ben Jonson write the _____ that is engraved on Shakespeare's tombstone?

9. The Planning Board refused to allow the construction of a factory in close _____ to our school building.

10. The "ghostly figure" you think you saw in the graveyard was no more than a(n) _____ created by your imagination.

11. Regulation of radio and TV stations falls within the _____ of the Federal Government.

12. I hope he was just being _____ when he said that my dancing reminded him of a trained bear.

13. Although nature has been far from _____ with its gifts to Japan, that nation has become highly productive and prosperous.

14. In answer to unfair criticisms, we _____ proudly that Americans have been most generous in giving aid to the needy.

15. The movie about invaders from outer space was so successful that the studio is preparing a(n) _____ .

16. In that elegant French restaurant, serving all kinds of fancy foods, Alice ordered a(n) _____ ham and cheese on rye (with mustard).

17. People of all religions strive to live up to the _____ standards summarized in the Ten Commandments.

18. Although they did not dare to attack the emperor's favorite publicly, they _____ in secret to bring about his downfall.

19. Since the public-address system was not working, the voice of the speaker was completely _____ to most of the people in the hall.

20. Since you were given _____ time to prepare your report, I can see no excuse for your failure to complete it.

Synonyms *From the words for this unit, choose the one that is most nearly **the same** in meaning as each of the following groups of expressions. Write the word on the line given.*

1. comical, witty, tongue-in-cheek _____

2. to grind, pound, crush, demolish _____

3. an area of authority or control, purview _____

4. a follow-up, continuation _____

5. a scheme, plot, conspiracy _____

6. lowborn, proletarian; coarse, unrefined _____

7. incapable of being heard _____

8. unstable, erratic; explosive _____

9. to declare, affirm, avow   _____

10. to cringe, flinch   _____

11. nearness in time or place   _____

12. a tombstone inscription   _____

13. a phantom, specter   _____

14. haphazard, random; unselective, uncritical   _____

15. contempt; to scorn, spurn, reject   _____

16. moral, upright, virtuous, honorable   _____

17. believable, probable, reasonable   _____

18. wasteful, improvident; lavish; spendthrift, wastrel   _____

19. shocked, horrified, stupefied   _____

20. sufficient, adequate, considerable   _____

Antonyms   *From the words for this unit, choose the one that is most nearly **opposite** in meaning to each of the following groups of expressions. Write the word on the line given.*

1. to revere, venerate, esteem, respect   _____

2. serious, humorless   _____

3. aristocratic; refined, cultivated   _____

4. fair play, dealings that are out in the open and aboveboard   _____

5. selective, discriminating, judicious   _____

6. improbable, far-fetched   _____

7. stable, steady; static, inert, dormant   _____

8. to stand up to, refuse to back down   _____

9. immoral, unscrupulous, dishonest   _____

10. insufficient, inadequate   _____

11. easily heard   _____

12. distance, remoteness   _____

13. frugal, economical; stingy, miserly   _____

14. a prelude, overture, curtain-raiser   _____

15. delighted, overjoyed; unmoved   _____

5

Choosing the Right Word   *Encircle the **boldface** word that more satisfactorily completes each of the following sentences.*

1. During the crisis, the (**apparition, proximity**) of nuclear war between the superpowers once again raised its ugly head.

2. When Jim missed practice for two days, he never thought that the (**sequel, disdain**) to this would be dismissal from the team.

3. His explanation that he is failing math because "the teacher is down on me" doesn't seem (**plausible, volatile**).

4. His furniture is supposed to be "original" and "colorful," but I think it is a(n) (**indiscriminate, facetious**) collection of junk.

5. You can show respect for your supervisors without seeming to (**assert, cower**) whenever one of them speaks to you.

6. Only a foolish snob would show such (**disdain, intrigue**) for anyone who doesn't belong to a country club.

7. In the years ahead, we may be forced to make more use of our (**ample, plebeian**) coal resources to meet our growing energy needs.

8. Finally the voters, (**volatile, aghast**) that such scandalous goings-on could have occurred in their town, demanded the mayor's immediate resignation.

9. We Americans do not believe that people who come from poor families should be regarded as (**plebeians, apparitions**).

10. The (**proximity, epitaph**) of the two men's ideas on many subjects made it easy for them to work together during that critical period of our history.

11. Your thoughtless remarks hurt me deeply, even though you say that you were merely trying to be (**ethical, facetious**).

12. Vic's moods are so (**ample, volatile**) that we never know if he will be in a good humor or down in the dumps.

13. Deciding who is or isn't eligible for school athletic teams is not within the (**jurisdiction, proximity**) of the Student Council.

14. It will take the two of us months of strict economizing to make up for that one (**prodigal, ethical**) shopping spree.

15. I find Margit's way of speaking English and her stories about her native Denmark most (**plebeian, intriguing**).

16. I thought that my whispers to Jan were (**prodigal, inaudible**), but I learned otherwise when Mr. Ferner told me in no uncertain terms to be quiet.

17. The purpose of this experiment is to find out whether a substance will dissolve more rapidly in water if it is thoroughly (**disdained, pulverized**).

18. A lawyer may be punished by disbarment if it can be shown that he has violated the (**ethics, jurisdiction**) of the legal profession.

19. Although I may not agree with what you have to say, I will always (**assert, disdain**) your right to say it.

20. "He tried hard, but he didn't have what it takes"—these words might serve as his (**epitaph, sequel**).

Definitions *Note carefully the spelling, pronunciation, and definition of each of the following words. Then write the word in the blank space in the illustrative phrase following.*

1. abashed
(ə 'basht)
(*adj., part.*) embarrassed or ashamed

_____ by his mistake

2. aloof
(ə 'lüf)
(*adj.*) withdrawn, standing apart from others (usually as a matter of choice)

kept _____ from his coworkers

3. anguish
('aŋ gwish)
(*n.*) great suffering, distress, or pain; (*v.*) to be deeply tormented by pain or sorrow

suffered great mental _____

4. articulate
(*v.*, är 'tik yü lāt;
adj., är 'tik yə lit)
(*v.*) to pronounce distinctly; to express well in words; to fit together into a system; (*adj.*) able to use language effectively; expressed clearly and forcefully

an _____ speaker

5. bask
(bask)
(*v.*) to be in, or expose oneself to, pleasant warmth; to take pleasure or derive enjoyment from

_____ in the sun

6. defect
(*n.*, 'dē fekt;
v., di 'fekt)
(*n.*) an imperfection or flaw of some kind; (*v.*) to desert a cause or organization

the grave _____ in his character

7. finesse
(fi 'nes)
(*n.*) delicate skill; tact and cleverness; (*v.*) to accomplish something by cleverness, good judgment, or skillful evasion

_____ in handling a situation

8. flaunt
(flônt)
(*v.*) to wave or flutter showily; to display in a conceited, offensive way

_____ one's riches in public

9. forthright
('fôrth rīt)
(*adj., adv.*) frank, direct, straightforward

stated in a very _____ way

10. genial
('jēn yəl)
(*adj.*) cordial, pleasantly cheerful or warm

a _____ household

11. instill
(in 'stil)
(*v.*) to add gradually; to introduce or cause to be taken in

_____ a love for reading in their children

12. ostracize
('äs trə sīz)
(*v.*) to exclude from a group, banish, send away

_____ bigots

13. premonition
(prē mə 'nish ən)

(*n.*) a forewarning or foreboding of a future event

a vague _____ of danger

14. pseudonym
('sü də nim)

(*n.*) a pen name, name assumed by a writer

a writer better known by her_____

15. purge
(pərj)

(*v.*) to wash away impurities, clean up; (*n.*) the process of getting rid of something or someone decisively

_____ oneself of prejudice

16. rehabilitate
(rē hə 'bil ə tāt)

(*v.*) to make over in good form; to restore to good condition or to a former position

try to _____ drug addicts

17. repercussion
(rē pər 'kəsh ən)

(*n.*) an effect or consequence of some action or event; an echo or reverberation

a policy that had unexpected _____

18. resolute
('rez ə lüt)

(*adj.*) bold, determined; firm

remain _____ despite setbacks

19. retentive
(ri 'tent iv)

(*adj.*) able to hold or keep; retaining knowledge easily

blessed with a _____memory

20. scapegoat
('skāp gōt)

(*n.*) a person or thing carrying the blame for others

refuse to be made the _____

Completing the Sentence

From the words for this unit, choose the one that best completes each of the following sentences. Write the word in the space provided.

1. Since we all know that Claire sings and plays the piano beautifully, what need is there for her to _____ her musical talents?

2. She has such a(n) _____ mind that she seems to master complicated details even without taking notes.

3. Even though I assured my dying grandfather that I would visit him soon, I had a strange _____ that I would never see him again.

4. Good citizens don't try to remain _____ from the problems and troubles in their communities.

5. The star basketball player _____ in the admiration of every small boy in the neighborhood.

6. I criticize Tom not because he makes mistakes but because he constantly looks for a(n) _____ to take the blame for them.

7. In recent years, pollution of our waterways has had serious and sometimes fatal _____ on the wildlife that inhabits them.

8. We learned that beneath the old man's quiet and withdrawn manner, there was a charming and _____ personality.

9. I have learned over the years that it is often possible to accomplish more by _____ than by brute force.

10. It took four years of civil war to _____ this nation of the curse of slavery.

11. Although every form of government has its _____ , democracy has more pluses and fewer minuses than any other.

12. Mr. Braun was found not guilty at his trial, but his punishment came when he was _____ by all his friends.

13. Can anything equal the _____ of a mother at the death of her child?

14. After the infamous attack on Pearl Harbor, the American people were _____ in their aim to defeat the fascist powers.

15. Although Hal was the only boy at the party wearing sneakers and an old sweatshirt, he did not seem at all _____ .

16. I think you will know who William S. Porter was if I tell you that he used the _____ O. Henry.

17. The city planner said that in addition to building new housing, we should plan to _____ many old buildings.

18. Instead of a(n) _____ answer, all we got from him was, "In one sense yes, but on the other hand perhaps no."

19. The speaker could not be understood easily because he swallowed his words instead of _____ them clearly.

20. By the example of his own conduct, Dad _____ in us a deep respect for people of all races, nationalities, and religions.

Synonyms *From the words for this unit, choose the one that is most nearly **the same** in meaning as each of the following groups of expressions. Write the word on the line given.*

1. friendly, warm, amiable _____

2. to cast out, expel, blackball, snub _____

3. a consequence or result _____

4. to cleanse, purify _____

5. steadfast, firm; determined, unflinching _____

6. to implant, infuse, inculcate _____

7. frank, candid, blunt; straightforward _____

8. ashamed, embarrassed, nonplussed _____

9. skill, delicacy _____

10. a fall guy, whipping boy _____

11. to enunciate, expound; glib, eloquent _____

12. to show off, parade _____

13. distant, cold, withdrawn, standoffish _____

14. able to hold or recall _____

15. a flaw, imperfection, blemish _____

16. to take pleasure in, wallow in, revel in _____

17. a pen name, nom de plume _____

18. a foreboding, presentiment _____

19. distress, mental suffering, misery _____

20. to reclaim, rebuild; to reform _____

Antonyms *From the words for this unit, choose the one that is most nearly **opposite** in meaning to each of the following groups of expressions. Write the word on the line given.*

1. to fraternize with, associate with _____

2. a cause or source _____

3. cold, unfriendly, unsociable _____

4. indirect, evasive; deceitful, two-faced _____

5. unembarrassed, unashamed _____

6. to hide, keep under wraps, downplay _____

7. porous; forgetful _____

8. involved, in the thick of things _____

9. weak, spineless, indecisive _____

10. clumsiness, awkwardness _____

11. tongue-tied; mumbled, incoherent _____

12. joy, delight; peace of mind _____

13. to pollute, contaminate, defile _____

14. to root out, eradicate, extirpate _____

44

Choosing the Right Word   *Encircle the **boldface** word that more satisfactorily completes each of the following sentences.*

1. Can we ever forgive him for (**defecting, purging**) from our great cause at the very time we needed him most!

2. An actor who has (**basked, abashed**) for so long in the favor of the public finds it hard to realize that he is no longer popular.

3. It will be better if we all take responsibility for the mistake instead of letting one employee be the (**pseudonym, scapegoat**).

4. We should now be just as (**resolute, retentive**) in fighting for peace as the Americans of two hundred years ago were in fighting for independence.

5. He's a clever man who has managed to (**anguish, finesse**) his way into a very important position in this company.

6. Is it our duty to try to (**flaunt, instill**) a faith in democracy in the people of other lands?

7. I did not think that such an innocent conversation could have such serious (**repercussions, pseudonyms**) on the outcome of an election.

8. Although Ed was trying to look unconcerned, I could see that he was much (**abashed, aloof**) by the teacher's criticism.

9. Shakespeare tries to convey Brutus's (**defects, premonitions**) of defeat at Philippi by having Caesar's ghost appear to him the night before the battle.

10. Fortunately, the soil is so (**resolute, retentive**) of moisture that the weeks of dry weather did not damage our crops.

11. He has lived (**aloof, abashed**) from other people for so long that it is hard for him to take part in everyday social affairs.

12. No matter how much time or effort it takes, I will (**purge, instill**) myself of these unfair charges of disloyalty!

13. It is possible to be honest and (**forthright, abashed**) in stating your views and opinions without being cruel or tactless.

14. The purpose of our prison system is not just to punish offenders but to (**rehabilitate, flaunt**) them.

15. My (**anguish, finesse**) at the loss of a loved one was all the greater when I realized that my carelessness had caused the accident.

16. His prejudices are so strong that he wants to (**ostracize, rehabilitate**) anyone who belongs to a minority religious group.

17. The new Governor's address was an unusually (**articulate, retentive**) and effective description of the challenges facing the state in the years ahead.

18. Jerry is not the most (**retentive, genial**) person in the world, but in his own way he is at least trying to be friendly.

19. Many female authors once used (**repercussions, pseudonyms**) because it was considered "improper" for women to write novels.

20. It would be good taste on his part not to (**flaunt, ostracize**) all the honors and awards that he has won.

Analogies   *In each of the following, encircle the item that best completes the comparison.*

1. **inaudible** is to **hear** as
a. inflammable is to feel
b. invisible is to see
c. indiscriminate is to touch
d. inaccurate is to smell

2. **sequel** is to **after** as
a. residue is to behind
b. proximity is to before
c. premonition is to between
d. intrigue is to beyond

3. **assert** is to **forward** as
a. obsess is to back
b. bask is to forward
c. cower is to back
d. deplore is to forward

4. **confirm** is to **invalidate** as
a. rehabilitate is to control
b. disdain is to scorn
c. peruse is to struggle
d. squander is to amass

5. **aghast** is to **horror** as
a. blasé is to enthusiasm
b. plausible is to resentment
c. abashed is to shame
d. aloof is to anguish

6. **purge** is to **oust** as
a. sustain is to support
b. instill is to remove
c. bolster is to delay
d. pulverize is to cement

7. **articulate** is to **voice** as
a. disdain is to nose
b. bask is to ears
c. instill is to mouth
d. peruse is to eyes

8. **epitaphs** are to **tombstones** as
a. graffiti are to walls
b. paintings are to galleries
c. ads are to newspapers
d. words are to phrases

9. **proximity** is to **close** as
a. recourse is to far
b. ampleness is to narrow
c. aloofness is to distant
d. premonition is to wide

10. **pain** is to **anguish** as
a. grief is to intrigue
b. appetite is to hunger
c. pleasure is to delight
d. fear is to disdain

11. **forthright** is to **favorable** as
a. plausible is to unfavorable
b. volatile is to favorable
c. frivolous is to unfavorable
d. plebeian is to favorable

12. **coward** is to **cower** as
a. champion is to ostracize
b. clown is to anguish
c. bully is to defect
d. showoff is to flaunt

13. **premonition** is to **before** as
a. epitaph is to back
b. repercussion is to after
c. prologue is to later
d. overture is to behind

14. **instill** is to **add** as
a. bolster is to subtract
b. oust is to add
c. purge is to subtract
d. ostracize is to add

15. **facetious** is to **serious** as
a. solicitous is to unconcerned
b. staid is to dignified
c. volatile is to daring
d. retentive is to memorable

16. **miser** is to **prodigal** as
a. scapegoat is to ornate
b. spendthrift is to frugal
c. apparition is to solicitous
d. friend is to genial

17. **pseudonym** is to **writer** as
a. surname is to family
b. alias is to criminal
c. nickname is to Michael
d. stage name is to painter

18. **prone** is to **upright** as
a. porous is to retentive
b. staid is to conservative
c. volatile is to explosive
d. resolute is to determined

Identification *In each of the following groups, encircle the word that is best defined or suggested by the introductory phrase.*

1. act as though nothing impresses or pleases them
a. blasé   b. resolute   c. volatile   d. porous

2. taking pleasure in the admiration of her classmates
a. flaunt   b. pulverize   c. bask   d. purge

3. always blaming everything on poor old Pete
a. premonition   b. scapegoat   c. aloof   d. sequel

4. handled the situation like a skilled diplomat
a. plebeian   b. scapegoat   c. solicitous   d. finesse

5. Hamlet sees the ghost of his murdered father.
a. proximity   b. apparition   c. qualm   d. bolster

6. a mother who is constantly worried about her child
a. staid   b. aloof   c. solicitous   d. aghast

7. gave a boost to their drooping spirits
a. sustain   b. bolster   c. peruse   d. deplore

8. "I'm not at all sure I did the right thing."
a. qualms   b. sequels   c. purges   d. scapegoats

9. what little remains after all the debts have been paid
a. nonentity   b. epitaph   c. anguish   d. residue

10. a candidate who tells us openly just what she thinks
a. genial   b. forthright   c. resolute   d. finesse

11. a quiet girl who hates to attract attention
a. staid   b. volatile   c. ethical   d. plebeian

12. "Our new car has a faulty windshield wiper."
a. intrigue   b. pseudonym   c. epitaph   d. defect

13. how most people feel about prejudice
a. bolster   b. sustain   c. assert   d. deplore

14. having a good memory for facts and figures
a. retentive   b. solicitous   c. inaudible   d. aghast

15. wrote another book about the same characters
a. proximity   b. sequel   c. jurisdiction   d. purge

16. had a strange feeling that something terrible was about to happen
a. purge   b. repercussion   c. residue   d. premonition

17. wrote under the pen name of Mark Twain
a. pseudonym   b. promontory   c. nonentity   d. defect

18. read the legal document with great care
a. obsess   b. peruse   c. cower   d. sequel

19. declare that the contract is no longer in effect
a. annul   b. sustain   c. deplore   d. pulverize

20. unable to talk or think about anything but the Senior Dance
a. sustained   b. rehabilitated   c. ousted   d. obsessed

R

Shades of Meaning

Read each sentence carefully. Then encircle the item that best completes the statement below the sentence.

Some scholars believe that the "Catalog of Ships" in the *Iliad* reproduces the official musters of the Greek forces that actually fought at Troy. **(2)**

1. The word **musters** in line 2 is used to mean
   a. gatherings   b. payrolls   c. rosters   d. biographies

The judge quickly sustained the defense's objection to the DA's question as "irrelevant and incompetent." **(2)**

2. In line 1 the word **sustained** most nearly means
   a. nourished   c. withstood
   b. validated   d. underwent

"No, we didn't just beat our opponents," she replied scornfully; "we pulverized them, 56-zip!" **(2)**

3. The best meaning for the word **pulverized** in line 2 is
   a. pummeled   c. overcame
   b. ground   d. demolished

Since 1938 the Federal Food and Drug Administration has regulated the manufacture, distribution, and sale of ethical drugs like insulin and nonprescription products like aspirin. **(2)**

4. In line 2 the word **ethical** is best defined as
   a. legal   c. morally permissible
   b. requiring a prescription   d. pure

One of the jobs a paleontologist performs involves articulating the fossil remains of animals that have been extinct for millennia. **(2)**

5. The word **articulating** in line 1 most nearly means
   a. fitting together   c. expressing
   b. pronouncing   d. clarifying

Antonyms

*In each of the following groups, encircle the item that is most nearly the **opposite** of the first word in **boldface type**.*

1. peruse
a. play
b. skim
c. return
d. study

2. ample
a. tall
b. full
c. inadequate
d. outstanding

3. frivolous
a. plain
b. serious
c. loud
d. poor

4. proximity
a. dullness
b. danger
c. damage
d. distance

5. aloof
a. low
b. involved
c. careful
d. meek

6. resolute
a. secret
b. quiet
c. hesitant
d. difficult

7. defect
a. remain faithful
b. betray
c. admire
d. organize

8. staid
a. movable
b. flashy
c. clean
d. pretty

9. abashed	12. prone	15. blasé	18. ornate
a. elderly	a. careful	a. willful	a. common
b. unashamed	b. possible	b. enthusiastic	b. wrong
c. cheap	c. unlikely	c. plain	c. simple
d. whole	d. thoughtless	d. empty	d. kind
10. volatile	**13. annul**	**16. plebeian**	**19. articulate**
a. unsafe	a. concern	a. ugly	a. touch
b. helpful	b. reduce	b. aristocratic	b. mumble
c. depressed	c. embarrass	c. brave	c. persuade
d. stable	d. confirm	d. safe	d. collect
11. forthright	**14. porous**	**17. nonentity**	**20. aghast**
a. full	a. rich	a. officer	a. frightened
b. indirect	b. likely	b. player	b. horrified
c. selective	c. solid	c. celebrity	c. youthful
d. ashamed	d. disturbed	d. victim	d. delighted

Completing the Sentence   *From the following words, choose the one that best completes each of the sentences below. Write the word in the appropriate space.*

Group A

ornate	sequel	blasé	oust
indiscriminate	pulverize	abashed	solicitous
qualm	defect	obsess	plebeian

1. Her reading is so _____ that it ranges from Shakespeare to comic books.

2. "I just don't think that _____ Victorian armchair with all the 'gingerbread' on it goes very well with our Danish modern interior," she said.

3. Under the City Charter, the voters can _____ any officials whom they consider unworthy of their jobs.

4. As we won one game after another, the entire school became almost _____ with the idea of an unbeaten season.

5. In spite of all his wealth, his tastes are so _____ that he lives like an ordinary worker.

Group B

aloof	volatile	deplore	ethical
articulate	peruse	proximity	recourse
plausible	sustain	muster	promontory

1. I never grow tired of the magnificent scene I behold when I stand on the _____ and look out to sea.

2. "Is it _____ ," asked the defense attorney, "that my client was at the scene of the crime without anyone seeing him there?"

3. We all _____ pollution of the environment, but are we doing anything effective to prevent it?

4. Even though he was the center of the controversy, Charles Bon remained somehow curiously _____ from it, as if it were happening to some third party and not himself.

5. If you are not sure of the meaning of a word you wish to use, you should have _____ to a good dictionary.

Word Families

A. On the line provided, write a **noun form** of each of the following words.

EXAMPLE: ornate — **ornateness**

1. frivolous _____

2. assert _____

3. genial _____

4. ample _____

5. plausible _____

6. peruse _____

7. resolute _____

8. porous _____

9. rehabilitate _____

10. annul _____

11. ostracize _____

B. On the line provided, write a **verb form** of each of the following words.

EXAMPLE: abashed — **abash**

1. deplorable _____

2. ostracism _____

3. rehabilitation _____

4. disdainful _____

5. obsessively _____

6. purgatory _____

7. retentive _____

8. assertive _____

9. pulverization _____

10. resolute _____

**Filling
the Blanks**

*Encircle the pair of words that best complete the
meaning of each of the following sets of sentences.*

1. "His cold and distant attitude toward people clearly betrays his deep
   _____ of the human race," I observed. "No one who
   genuinely likes human beings would constantly prefer to remain so
   _____ from them."
   a. apparition . . . solicitous
   b. disdain . . . aloof
   c. anguish . . . prone
   d. obsession . . . abashed

2. Since her objections to the plan were clearly _____ , I
   thought that she was being _____ . After all, if she had
   been serious, her comments would have had more substance to them.
   a. plausible . . . articulate
   b. genial . . . solicitous
   c. inaudible . . . forthright
   d. frivolous . . . facetious

3. "Using a(n) _____ has caused me a really unexpected
   problem," the famous novelist remarked. "Most people only know me by
   my pen name. So, if I introduce myself by my real name, I run the risk of
   being regarded as a complete _____ ."
   a. pseudonym . . . nonentity
   b. bolster . . . scapegoat
   c. sequel . . . plebeian
   d. epitaph . . . apparition

4. Elected officials cannot be too careful about their behavior while in office. If
   they become _____ about matters of right and wrong, they
   may do things that the average citizen of this country does not consider
   _____ . Such mistakes could cost the offenders their jobs.
   a. solicitous . . . plausible
   b. obsessed . . . prodigal
   c. blasé . . . ethical
   d. resolute . . . indiscriminate

5. Some of my friends have remarkably _____ memories from
   which nothing ever seems to escape. Unfortunately, I've been blessed with
   a memory that is as _____ as a sieve.
   a. staid . . .durable
   b. retentive . . . porous
   c. ample . . . volatile
   d. devoid . . . prodigious

6. Though I tried to _____ my words clearly and distinctly, my
   voice was all but _____ above the roar of the storm.
   a. sustain . . .ample
   b. bolster . . . abashed
   c. articulate . . . inaudible
   d. muster . . . prone

7. During the bloody _____ of the early 1930s, Josef Stalin
   "liquidated" every potential rival whom he feared might one day seek to
   _____ him from his position as absolute master.
   a. purges . . . oust
   b. repercussions . . .sustain
   c. premonitions . . . ostracize
   d. sequels . . . intrigue

Analogies *In each of the following, encircle the letter of the item that best completes the comparison.*

1. troops are to **muster** as
a. market is to glut
b. effort is to sustain
c. money is to amass
d. riot is to instigate

2. ample is to **bountiful** as
a. porous is to watertight
b. lacking is to devoid
c. aloof is to solicitous
d. volatile is to hysterical

3. frugal is to **prodigal** as
a. myriad is to complex
b. wanton is to willful
c. prodigious is to legendary
d. staid is to flamboyant

4. audacious is to **cower** as
a. timid is to tremble
b. obstinate is to yield
c. inaudible is to hear
d. enterprising is to venture

5. annul is to **invalidate** as
a. purge is to purify
b. minimize is to exaggerate
c. pulverize is to vie
d. comply is to request

6. collaborators are to **cooperate** as
a. friends are to wrangle
b. scapegoats are to obsess
c. conspirators are to intrigue
d. apparitions are to flaunt

7. plebeians are to **elite** as
a. voters are to electorate
b. relatives are to family
c. industrialists are to economy
d. outcasts are to society

8. churlish is to **genial** as
a. saucy is to abashed
b. heavy is to gingerly
c. tardy is to laggard
d. relevant is to plausible

9. citadel is to **city** as
a. promontory is to sea
b. vigil is to night
c. rubble is to explosion
d. perspective is to painting

10. inhibited is to **qualms** as
a. retentive is to memories
b. indiscriminate is to standards
c. skittish is to reservations
d. resolute is to misgivings

Shades of Meaning *Read each sentence carefully. Then encircle the item that best completes the statement below the sentence.*

What would our "Wild, Wild West" have been without those hordes of ranch hands punching cows and wrangling horses? **(2)**

1. The word **wrangling** in line 2 is best defined as
a. rustling
b. arguing with
c. herding
d. raising

The enduring wonder of the King James Version of the Bible is that so frugal a vocabulary can express such complex ideas so memorably. **(2)**

2. In line 2 the word **frugal** most nearly means
a. ordinary
b. skimpy
c. unusual
d. limited

Unlike the "decrees" of the skittish world of high fashion, the laws of nature never change. **(2)**

3. In line 1 the word **skittish** most nearly means
a. fickle
b. bashful
c. cautious
d. coy

Our opponent's defense was so porous that we had little trouble scoring points against it either on the ground or in the air. **(2)**

4. The word **porous** in line 1 is best defined as
   a. disorganized
   b. permeable
   c. inexperienced
   d. cautious

Our troupe called its version of the age-old morality tale "The Prodigal" so it would not be confused with a Prokofiev ballet on the same subject. **(2)**

5. In line 1 the word **Prodigal** is best defined as
   a. Genius
   b. Liberal
   c. Openhanded
   d. Wastrel

Filling the Blanks

Encircle the pair of words that best complete the meaning of each of the following sentences.

1. Like so many moths around a lamp, team doctors and field attendants _____ anxiously over the _____ figure of the injured player sprawled on the 50-yard line.
   a. jostled . . . laggard
   b. hovered . . . prone
   c. basked . . . prodigious
   d. wrangled . . . dissonant

2. Modern-day teachers still use such time-honored _____ as "Early to bed, early to rise, makes a man healthy, wealthy, and wise" to _____ desirable personal qualities in the minds of their students.
   a. epitaphs . . . bolster
   b. excerpts . . . instigate
   c. adages . . . instill
   d. antics . . . articulate

3. On the night before the fateful battle, the general's normally placid mind was deeply _____ by ominous _____ of disaster, which unfortunately proved to be accurate.
   a. perturbed . . . premonitions
   b. obsessed . . . vigils
   c. anguished . . . myriads
   d. tethered . . . apparitions

4. Overproduction _____ the market with goods, which in turn caused prices to fall, lowered profit margins, and had several other severe _____ on the industry.
   a. sustained . . . residues
   b. glutted . . . repercussions
   c. pulverized . . . sequels
   d. congested . . . perspectives

5. As a(n) _____ enemy of all forms of social and political injustice, I believe it is my duty to _____ the rights of the downtrodden openly and without hesitation.
   a. solicitous . . . deplore
   b. durable . . . venerate
   c. resolute . . . allot
   d. avowed . . . assert

Unit 7

Definitions

Note carefully the spelling, pronunciation, and definition of each of the following words. Then write the word in the blank space in the illustrative phrase following.

1. **acme**
   ('ak mē)

   (*n.*) the highest point

   the _____ of success

2. **attribute**
   (*n.*, 'at trə byüt;
   v., ə 'trib yət)

   (*n.*) a quality or characteristic belonging to or associated with someone or something; (*v.*) to assign to, credit with; to regard as caused by or resulting from

   a painting _____ to Rembrandt

3. **belittle**
   (bi 'lit əl)

   (*v.*) to make something appear smaller than it is; to refer to in a way that suggests lack of importance or value

   _____ my ability

4. **convey**
   (kən 'vā)

   (*v.*) to transport; to transmit; to communicate, make known; to transfer ownership or title to

   _____ our best wishes

5. **doctrine**
   ('däk trin)

   (*n.*) a belief, principle, or teaching; a system of such beliefs or principles; a formulation of such beliefs or principles

   the _____ of free enterprise

6. **excise**
   (*v.*, ek 'sīz;
   n., 'ek sīz)

   (*v.*) to remove by cutting; (*n.*) an indirect tax on the manufacture, sale, or distribution of a commodity or service

   _____ an irrelevant paragraph

7. **exotic**
   (ig 'zät ik)

   (*adj.*) foreign; charmingly unfamiliar or strikingly unusual

   a rare and _____ bird

8. **haggard**
   ('hag ərd)

   (*adj.*) thin, pale, and careworn as a result of worry or suffering; wild-looking

   startled by his _____ appearance

9. **jaunty**
   ('jôn tē)

   (*adj.*) lively, easy, and carefree (in manner); smart or trim (in appearance)

   walk with a _____ step

10. **juncture**
    ('jungk chər)

    (*n.*) a joining together; the point at which two things are joined; any important point in time

    at the _____ of the two walls

11. **menial**
    ('mē nē əl)

    (*adj.*) lowly, humble, lacking importance or dignity; (*n.*) a servant who does the humble and unpleasant tasks

    find no task too _____

12. **parry**
    ('par ē)

    (*v.*) to ward off, evade, avoid; (*n.*) a defensive movement in fencing and other sports

    _____ all questions

13. predatory
('pred ə tôr ē)

(*adj.*) preying on, plundering, or piratical

hawks and other _____ birds

14. ravage
('rav ij)

(*v.*) to destroy, lay waste, ruin; (*n.*) ruinous damage, destruction

a country _____ by war

15. stance
(stans)

(*n.*) a way of holding the body; an attitude or position on an issue

changed his _____

16. tawdry
('tô drē)

(*adj.*) showy and flashy but lacking in good taste

a _____ costume

17. turncoat
('tərn kōt)

(*n.*) a person who switches to an opposing side or party

have only contempt for the _____

18. unassuming
(ən ə 'sü miŋ)

(*adj.*) not putting on airs, modest

an _____ personality

19. wallow
('wäl ō)

(*v.*) to roll about in a lazy, clumsy, or helpless way; to overindulge in; to have in abundance; (*n.*) a wet, muddy, or dusty area used by animals as a sort of bath; a state of moral or physical collapse

_____ in money

20. waver
('wā vər)

(*v.*) to move to and fro, become unsteady; to show lack of firmness or decision

wheat that _____ in the breeze

Completing the Sentence

From the words for this unit, choose the one that best completes each of the following sentences. Write the word in the space provided.

1. Even though you start at a(n) _____ job, you may gain valuable experience and move upward rapidly.

2. The Nobel Prize winner was so _____ that we took him to be just another struggling writer attending the conference.

3. He sat there staring at the menu, _____ between the steak sandwich and the chef's salad.

4. Though many _____ creatures prefer to hunt at night, lions and leopards are active during the daytime.

5. During her trip through Kenya, my cousin took pictures of hippos as they _____ in a mudhole.

6. When he switched parties, people called him a(n) _____ , but he said that he had just had an honest change of opinion.

7. Since my boss has, as they say, "a short fuse," patience cannot be considered one of his outstanding _____ .

8. Two of our divisions were marching rapidly towards each other and hoped to effect a(n) _____ before the enemy attacked.

9. Disease had so _____ his once handsome face that I could scarcely recognize him!

10. The Monroe _____ sought to prevent the colonization of the American continents by European powers.

11. Her happy expression and the _____ way she walked down the street gave the impression of someone "on top of the world."

12. The drawn and _____ faces of the rescued miners showed clearly the terrible strain they had undergone.

13. In her most celebrated novels, such as *Pride and Prejudice* and *Emma*, Jane Austen reached the _____ of her literary art.

14. Because of his ability to _____ his opponents' blows, he was rarely hurt in his many fights in the ring.

15. We will need several trucks to _____ all the books to the new library building.

16. Because Ted Williams was one of the greatest hitters of all time, many batters have tried to imitate his _____ at the plate.

17. The room was so overcrowded with flashy furnishings that the overall effect was cheap and _____ .

18. I agree that we should not exaggerate his achievements, but we should not _____ them either.

19. In the early 19th century, Thomas Bowdler attempted to "clean up" the works of Shakespeare by _____ all words and phrases that he felt were coarse or offensive.

20. Most Americans think of Australia as a strange and wonderful continent full of _____ plants and animals.

Synonyms   *From the words for this unit, choose the one that is most nearly **the same** in meaning as each of the following groups of expressions. Write the word on the line given.*

1. flashy, loud, garish, gaudy, tacky, vulgar   _____

2. a traitor, deserter, renegade   _____

3. to carry, transport; to send, transmit; to impart   _____

4. carefree, unconcerned, lighthearted   _____

56

5. to wreck, lay waste, devastate _____

6. strange, alien; picturesque, colorful _____

7. to hesitate, falter _____

8. careworn, drawn, gaunt, wasted _____

9. posture, bearing; a position _____

10. lowly, humble; a servant, underling, scullion _____

11. a principle, belief _____

12. to ward off, fend off, deflect _____

13. modest, unpretentious _____

14. looting, pillaging; ravenous, rapacious _____

15. to cut out, delete, expunge _____

16. a quality, trait; to credit with, ascribe to _____

17. to roll about; to delight in, bask in _____

18. a union; a seam, joint; a turning point _____

19. the summit, top, peak, pinnacle _____

20. to minimize, underrate, disparage _____

Antonyms From the words for this unit, choose the one that is most nearly **opposite** in meaning to each of the following groups of expressions. Write the word on the line given.

1. downcast, dejected, glum _____

2. to stand firm, be resolute _____

3. to put in, insert, interpolate _____

4. native, indigenous; familiar, commonplace _____

5. a loyalist, diehard _____

6. the low point, bottom, nadir _____

7. conceited, pretentious, self-important _____

8. refined, tasteful; subdued, muted _____

9. to exaggerate, magnify, overestimate _____

10. healthy, glowing, radiant, hale and hearty _____

11. a boss, master; lofty, elevated _____

12. to do no harm to, spare _____

Choosing the Right Word   *Encircle the **boldface** word that more satisfactorily completes each of the following sentences.*

1. Instead of answering my question, the skillful debater (**parried, ravaged**) by asking a question of his own.

2. Mother said that she certainly believes in the (**doctrine, acme**) of human brotherhood but would like to broaden it to include "human sisterhood."

3. He is so conceited that it is hard to (**convey, parry**) to him the simple idea that we don't want him as a member of our group.

4. For a long time the towns and villages of the Normandy coast of France showed the (**ravages, doctrines**) of the great invasion of 1944.

5. Americans expect candidates to take a definite (**stance, parry**) on each of the important issues in a national election.

6. The immigrants never (**excised, wavered**) in their determination to become American citizens.

7. No matter how (**menial, tawdry**) the assignment may be, take pride in your work, and do your best.

8. I am thoroughly disgusted by people who try to make themselves seem more important than they really are by (**conveying, belittling**) others.

9. While we were in the Orient, we sampled such (**exotic, predatory**) dishes as thousand-year-old eggs and bird's nest soup.

10. I could see that the captain was deeply worried, even though he tried hard to appear confident and (**haggard, jaunty**) to the passengers.

11. History teaches us that in any great crisis, there will be some (**turncoats, menials**) willing to go over to the enemy.

12. Even after pitching two no-hit games this season, Stan was the same quiet and (**jaunty, unassuming**) boy we had always known.

13. So long as you continue to (**parry, wallow**) in self-pity, you will lack the strength needed to solve your problems.

14. He hoped that election to the Presidency would be the (**acme, attribute**) of his long and brilliant career.

15. "If we are to keep the body politic healthy," the Senator remarked, "we must (**excise, attribute**) the cancer of racial prejudice entirely from it."

16. No wonder she looked careworn and (**haggard, jaunty**) after waiting for news of her loved ones for several days.

17. We were disgusted by the (**unassuming, tawdry**) speech in which he tried to present himself as a great national leader.

18. Thieves are essentially a (**predatory, jaunty**) class of criminals because they live off what they can take from others.

19. The general (**belittled, attributed**) our failure to win the battle to a lack of sufficient manpower rather than to a lack of courage.

20. When she arrived at that critical (**juncture, stance**) in her career, she realized that her whole future depended on the decision she made.

Unit 8

Definitions

Note carefully the spelling, pronunciation, and definition of each of the following words. Then write the word in the blank space in the illustrative phrase following.

1. abut
(ə 'bət)

(v.) to join at one end or next to; to support, prop up

houses that _____ the riverbank

2. attire
(ə 'tīr)

(n.) clothes, apparel; (v.) to dress or adorn

outfitted in expensive _____

3. avail
(ə 'vāl)

(v.) to be of use or benefit to; to make use of; (n.) use, benefit, or value

_____ themselves of the opportunity

4. crony
('krō nē)

(n.) a very close friend, pal, chum

surrounded by a group of _____

5. cryptic
('krip tik)

(adj.) puzzling or mystifying

send a _____ note

6. divergent
(də 'vər jənt)

(adj.) going in different directions; differing from each other; departing from convention, deviant

_____ interests

7. enmity
('en mə tē)

(n.) hatred, ill-will

felt _____ toward their conquerors

8. fervent
('fər vənt)

(adj.) very earnest, emotional, passionate; extremely hot

deliver a _____ plea for unity

9. gaunt
(gônt)

(adj.) thin and bony, starved looking; bare, barren

the _____ alley cat

10. infiltrate
('in fil trāt)

(v.) to pass through or gain entrance to gradually or stealthily

_____ enemy lines

11. nullify
('nəl ə fī)

(v.) to make of no value or consequence, cancel, wipe out

_____ a contract

12. perceptible
(pər 'sep tə bəl)

(adj.) capable of being grasped by the senses or mind

a _____ change in her appearance

13. plummet
('pləm ət)

(v.) to plunge straight down; (n.) a weight fastened to a line

_____ from the sky

14. proclaim
(prō 'klām)

(v.) to declare publicly or officially

_____ a state of war

15. proxy
('präk sē)

(n.) an agent, substitute; a written permission allowing one person to act in another's place

act as their _____

16. rankle
('raŋ kəl)

(v.) to cause anger, irritation, or bitterness (with the suggestion that the pain grows worse with time)

insults that _____ for many years

17. scavenger
('skav ən jər)

(n.) a person who collects or removes usable items from waste materials; an animal that feeds on refuse or dead bodies

jackals and other _____

18. stint
(stint)

(v.) to limit, be sparing or frugal; (n.) a limit or restriction; a fixed share of work or duty; a period of activity

_____ on their food

19. stoical
('stō i kəl)

(adj.) self-controlled, not showing feeling in response to pleasure or pain

_____ acceptance of misfortune

20. unflagging
(ən 'flag iŋ)

(adj.) tireless, continuing with vigor

_____ devotion to duty

Completing the Sentence

From the words for this unit, choose the one that best completes each of the following sentences. Write the word in the space provided.

1. I didn't think she would have the nerve to ask me for a loan, but she did it, and with no _____ embarrassment.

2. He tried to appear _____ when he heard the bad news, but I realized that he was deeply hurt.

3. Instead of giving us a clear answer, the speaker confined himself to the _____ prophecy that "time would tell."

4. His failure to win the election _____ in his mind until it caused a complete emotional breakdown.

5. As a youth he developed a(n) _____ interest in biology that led to a lifelong career.

6. Statements by witnesses are so _____ that it's hard to know how the accident actually happened.

7. The rise in the cost of living _____ my efforts to save some money from my small salary.

8. We decided not to buy the house, mainly because the property it stands on unfortunately _____ on the noisy main highway.

9. Since I will not be able to attend the meeting, I hereby appoint Mrs. Brown to act as my _____ .

10. Their parents had _____ for many years to save the money needed to send the children to college.

11. My father has three _____ who go with him each year on a camping trip in the High Sierras.

12. The vulture has a decidedly poor reputation, but it does a useful job as a(n) _____ , clearing away decaying materials.

13. Each year the President _____ the last Thursday in the month of November as a day of national thanksgiving.

14. To prepare for the job interview, she _____ herself in a neat, simple dress in quiet colors.

15. You will find it much easier to prepare a good term paper if in the future you _____ yourself of the services provided by the library.

16. Shakespeare said that Cassius had a "lean and hungry look," but I would describe him by the single word _____ .

17. We watched in horror as the airplane suddenly went out of control and _____ to earth.

18. In our community, people of many ethnic backgrounds work together without jealousy or _____ .

19. Even after he retired and we expected him to slow down, his efforts in support of his beloved school remained _____ .

20. Like thieves in the night, some of our men _____ the enemy's camp and captured their leader.

21. All her efforts to get more business for her troubled company proved to be of no _____ , and the store had to close down.

Synonyms   *From the words for this unit, choose the one that is most nearly **the same** in meaning as each of the following groups of expressions. Write the word on the line given.*

1. to slip into, creep into, penetrate   _____

2. enthusiastic, ardent; burning, blazing, scorching   _____

3. a deputy, representative   _____

4. to irritate, vex, nettle, irk, gall   _____

5. to announce, declare, promulgate   _____

6. steady, undiminished, unremitting   _____

7. hostility, animosity, antagonism _____

8. to limit, restrict; to scrimp, economize _____

9. to take a nosedive, plunge _____

10. to cancel, invalidate, annul _____

11. to profit, benefit; to take advantage of _____

12. noticeable, discernible, observable _____

13. lean, scrawny, lanky, all skin and bones _____

14. puzzling, mystifying, enigmatic _____

15. someone who rummages in waste _____

16. apparel, clothing, garb; to dress, bedeck _____

17. not in agreement, differing; unorthodox, unconventional _____

18. to border on, be next to; to bolster _____

19. self-controlled, unresponsive, impassive _____

20. a chum, pal, buddy _____

Antonyms *From the words for this unit, choose the one that is most nearly **opposite** in meaning to each of the following groups of expressions. Write the word on the line given.*

1. to soar, skyrocket _____

2. excitable, emotional, hotheaded _____

3. blasé, apathetic; restrained, emotionless _____

4. diminishing, drooping, sagging _____

5. to keep quiet about, conceal, cover up _____

6. to please, delight, gratify _____

7. merging, intersecting, converging; conventional, orthodox _____

8. plump, chubby, stout, corpulent _____

9. to confirm, endorse, ratify, sanction _____

10. crystal-clear, unambiguous _____

11. an enemy; a rival _____

12. friendship, amity _____

13. invisible, unnoticeable, indiscernible _____

14. to splurge, squander, lavish _____

Choosing the   *Encircle the **boldface** word that more satisfactorily*
Right Word   *completes each of the following sentences.*

1. It is a sad fact of experience that postwar political blunders can often (**nullify, infiltrate**) or even reverse the results of battlefield triumphs.

2. In a democracy, we expect people to have (**cryptic, divergent**) views and to express them openly.

3. Every day, the poor old man goes through all the litter baskets on our street, trying to make a living as a (**plummet, scavenger**).

4. I pretended that being ignored by the "best people in town" meant nothing to me, but actually those snubs (**rankled, nullified**) deeply.

5. After the big snowstorm, the trees seemed to be (**attired, scavenged**) in white lace.

6. It didn't take me long to master the (**cryptic, fervent**) greetings, signs, and handclasps that were part of the club's rituals.

7. Before going to college, Jack did a (**stint, proxy**) as an apprentice radio operator on an oceangoing tanker.

8. Let me state my unchanging (**enmity, stoicism**) for those who seek to bring about political change by violent means.

9. Our hopes for a winning touchdown (**plummeted, nullified**) in the last minute when Jim fumbled and South High recovered the ball.

10. President Kennedy bore his pain so (**stoically, perceptibly**) that few people realized how much he suffered from his World War II back injury.

11. We honor this wonderful woman tonight for her (**unflagging, divergent**) devotion to every good cause in our community.

12. The Senator shocked the nation with charges that Communists had (**infiltrated, stinted**) the various branches of our government.

13. The lost puppy was so happy to be home at last that he ran about the room licking everyone's hand (**fervently, perceptibly**).

14. If we had a good civil service system in this town, the mayor wouldn't be able to put his (**cronies, proxies**) on the public payroll.

15. Since the farmer's land (**abuts, stints**) a section of Interstate 95, he can get home at any time, even during deep snows.

16. In the unforgettable words of the Declaration of Independence, Jefferson (**proclaimed, rankled**) to the world that a new nation had been born.

17. All the heroism of our men could not (**avail, abut**) against the enemy's superior forces.

18. The (**gaunt, unflagging**) and leafless trees seemed to add to the gloom of that wintry scene.

19. Large numbers of stockholders sent in (**proxies, cronies**) allowing the directors of the corporation to vote for them.

20. The two candidates are working hard to get the voters' support, but in my opinion there is no (**cryptic, perceptible**) difference between them.

Unit 9

Definitions

Note carefully the spelling, pronunciation, and definition of each of the following words. Then write the word in the blank space in the illustrative phrase following.

1. apt
(apt)

(*adj.*) suitable, fitting, likely; quick to learn

proved to be an _____ pupil

2. awry
(ə 'rī)

(*adj., adv.*) in a turned or twisted position or direction; wrong, out of the right or hoped-for course

fear that the plan may go _____

3. bludgeon
('bləj ən)

(*n.*) a short club used as a weapon; (*v.*) to strike with a heavy club; to use force or strong arguments to gain some point

_____ the wild animal to death

4. capitulate
(kə 'pich ə lāt)

(*v.*) to end resistance, give up, surrender

_____ before his entire force was wiped out

5. chafe
(chāf)

(*v.*) to warm by rubbing; to wear sore by rubbing; to feel annoyance or dissatisfaction, annoy, irk; to strain or press against; (*n.*) a sore or injury caused by rubbing

had my neck _____

6. defile
(di 'fīl)

(*v., trans.*) to make unclean or dirty, destroy the purity of; (*v., intrans.*) to march in a single line or in columns; (*n.*) a narrow passage

_____ the house of worship

7. dire
(dīr)

(*adj.*) dreadful, causing fear or suffering; warning of trouble to come; demanding immediate action to avoid disaster

_____ consequences

8. disarming
(dis 'ärm iŋ)

(*adj.*) charming, tending to get rid of unfriendliness or suspicion

greet me with a _____ smile

9. disgruntled
(dis 'grənt əld)

(*part., adj.*) in bad humor, discontented, annoyed

_____ by the poor arrangement

10. encroach
(en 'krōch)

(*v.*) to advance beyond the usual or proper limits, trespass

planted hedges that _____ on our property

11. endow
(en 'daů)

(*v.*) to furnish, equip, provide with funds or some other desirable thing or quality

_____ the college

12. fend
(fend)

(*v.*) to ward off, resist; to get along, manage

tried to _____ off the attacking dog

13. impunity
(im 'pyü nə tē)

(*n.*) freedom from punishment

misbehave with _____

14. mien
(mēn)

(*n.*) air, manner; appearance; expression

have the _____ of a clergyman

15. penal
('pē nəl)

(*adj.*) having to do with punishment

_____ colonies like Devil's Island

16. pertinent
('pər tə nənt)

(*adj.*) related to the matter at hand, to the point

gather all the _____ information

17. predominant
(pri 'däm ə nənt)

(*adj.*) the greatest in strength or power; most common

the _____ figure in the business

18. prodigy
('präd ə jē)

(*n.*) something wonderful or marvelous; something monstrous or abnormal; an unusual feat; a child or young person with extraordinary ability or talent

an eight-year-old chess _____

19. recluse
('re klüs)

(*n.*) a person who leads a life shut up or withdrawn from the world

became a total _____

20. renown
(ri 'naun)

(*n.*) fame, glory

gained national _____

Completing the Sentence

From the words for this unit, choose the one that best completes each of the following sentences. Write the word in the space provided.

1. We were prepared to make an angry complaint to the salesclerk, but her

_____ manner soon put us in a more friendly mood.

2. To carry out his great work, he chose to separate himself from society and

live the solitary life of a(n) _____ .

3. Sideshow exhibits at the circus usually include mermaids, wolfmen, and

other so-called _____ of nature.

4. As the jurors filed back into the courtroom, their stern _____
alarmed the defendants.

5. She promised that she would not be the kind of meddling mother-in-law

who _____ on the privacy of her married children.

6. Even though you are _____ because the candidate you
favored did not win the nomination, you should still vote in the election.

7. True, I wanted to make some money, but my _____ reason for taking the job was that I needed practical work experience.

8. Even before Martin Luther King won the Nobel Peace Prize in 1964, his

_____ had spread throughout most of the world.

9. The Scottish poet Robert Burns reminds us that, no matter how carefully

we plan, things may still go _____ .

10. There's an old saying which tells us that if you walk like a duck and talk

like a duck, people are _____ to take you for a duck.

11. When his efforts to _____ off the angry bill collectors proved unsuccessful, my uncle was forced to leave town.

12. Let us hope that he is wrong in his _____ prediction that there will be a third world war.

13. We were amazed that the large, fierce-looking dog allowed the child to pull

his tail with _____ .

14. He has a decidedly unpleasant habit of using facts and figures like a(n)

_____ to beat down his opponents in an argument.

15. Do you believe that the crime rate will go down if the _____ code is made more severe?

16. In your answers, try to limit yourself to giving us only the details that you

know are _____ to this investigation.

17. Shoes that will not _____ your feet are the most important part of the equipment for a hike.

18. In my opinion, the countryside is _____ by billboards that block our view of the beauties of nature.

19. It is up to you to make good use of the talents with which nature has seen

fit to _____ you.

20. The brave soldiers defending the fort _____ only when they realized that further resistance was useless.

Synonyms *From the words for this unit, choose the one that is most nearly **the same** in meaning as each of the following groups of expressions. Write the word on the line given.*

1. a marvel, wonder; a freak; a genius   _____

2. look, expression; bearing, demeanor   _____

3. fame, reputation, celebrity, prestige   _____

4. chief, major, paramount; prevalent   _____

5. appropriate; fit, proper; liable   _____

6. a loner, hermit   _____

7. exemption from penalty, immunity   _____

8. charming, endearing, winning   _____

9. to pollute, contaminate; to desecrate; gorge, canyon   _____

10. to trespass, intrude, infringe   _____

11. a club, cudgel; to clobber, clout   _____

12. to ward off, stave off; to cope   _____

13. to irritate, irk; to scrape, abrade   _____

14. crooked, askew; amiss   _____

15. discontented, displeased; grumpy, surly   _____

16. correctional, disciplinary   _____

17. disastrous; ominous, sinister; urgent   _____

18. to give up, throw in the towel   _____

19. to grant, bestow, present, bequeath   _____

20. relevant, germane, apropos   _____

Antonyms   *From the words for this unit, choose the one that is most nearly **opposite** in meaning to each of the following groups of expressions. Write the word on the line given.*

1. secondary, minor, subsidiary; rare   _____

2. unrelated, irrelevant, immaterial   _____

3. obscurity; infamy, notoriety   _____

4. a dumbbell, dunce, dullard   _____

5. to take away, deprive   _____

6. pleased, satisfied, content   _____

7. alarming, troubling, disquieting   _____

8. to cleanse, purify   _____

9. to soothe, mollify; to please, elate   _____

10. to hold out, persist, go down fighting   _____

11. favorable, auspicious; beneficial   _____

12. inappropriate; unlikely; slow   _____

13. straight, symmetrical   _____

Choosing the Right Word *Encircle the **boldface** word that more satisfactorily completes each of the following sentences.*

1. A team as determined to win as ours is will never (**capitulate, encroach**), no matter how many points behind it is in the final moments of a game.

2. Nature is kind to us in many ways, but we must learn that we cannot violate nature's laws with (**impunity, recluse**).

3. The rights guaranteed us by the United States Constitution do not permit us to (**bludgeon, encroach**) on the rights of others.

4. The Declaration of Independence mentions a number of "unalienable rights" with which "men are (**endowed, renowned**) by their Creator."

5. During the winter the wind usually blows from the north in that area, but during the summer southerly currents are (**predominant, awry**).

6. The lecturer is a man who served ten years in prison and is now devoting his life to bringing about reforms in our (**penal, pertinent**) system.

7. The college my sister attends is a small one, but it has won a great deal of (**recluse, renown**) for the quality of its faculty.

8. When the featured singer failed to appear, the (**disgruntled, apt**) fans demanded their money back.

9. The way in which he asked for a loan was so (**disarming, chafing**) that almost to my surprise I found myself giving him the money.

10. My problem was to (**fend, bludgeon**) off their unwelcome attentions without being openly insulting.

11. He claims to be a patriot, but his appeals to racism are (**encroaching, defiling**) the great ideals on which this nation is built.

12. His modest dress and quiet (**recluse, mien**) were not what we expected in a famous Hollywood director.

13. Some great composers, such as Mozart and Mendelssohn, have shown an amazing (**pertinence, aptitude**) for music at a very early age.

14. Do you understand how someone can live as a (**mien, recluse**) even in the midst of a great city?

15. The joke she told was very amusing, but I fail to see how it is (**pertinent, disgruntled**) to the subject.

16. Yes, we are still friends, but not as close as we used to be; something has gone (**awry, dire**) in our friendship.

17. As we use up the earth's fossil-fuel supplies, we are faced with an increasingly (**disarming, dire**) need to develop new energy sources.

18. What bad taste it is for Ray to approach people he scarcely knows and (**bludgeon, chafe**) his way into private conversations!

19. The injured quarterback (**chafed, defiled**) at sitting on the bench while his team was being badly beaten on the field.

20. Alvin York performed such (**bludgeons, prodigies**) on the battlefields of France that he was awarded this nation's highest honors.

Review Units 7–9

Analogies   *In each of the following, encircle the item that best completes the comparison.*

1. thin is to **gaunt** as
a. dire is to weak
b. careless is to awry
c. tired is to exhausted
d. clear is to cryptic

2. crony is to **friendship** as
a. proxy is to enmity
b. turncoat is to betrayal
c. recluse is to renown
d. scapegoat is to impunity

3. acme is to **high** as
a. menial is to low
b. stance is to high
c. mien is to low
d. stint is to high

4. tawdry is to **unfavorable** as
a. predatory is to favorable
b. unflagging is to unfavorable
c. apt is to favorable
d. pertinent is to unfavorable

5. parry is to **blow** as
a. bludgeon is to club
b. fend off is to attack
c. chafe is to neck
d. ravage is to scavenger

6. neck is to **chafe** as
a. knife is to bludgeon
b. boredom is to yawn
c. sandpaper is to defile
d. shoe is to scuff

7. traitor is to **turncoat** as
a. hermit is to recluse
b. musician is to prodigy
c. enemy is to crony
d. judge is to criminal

8. suffering is to **haggard** as
a. enmity is to disarming
b. hesitation is to unflagging
c. contentment is to disgruntled
d. starvation is to gaunt

9. soar is to **plummet** as
a. attire is to adorn
b. ratify is to nullify
c. fend is to parry
d. stint is to abut

10. jaunty is to **good mood** as
a. disgruntled is to bad mood
b. irritated is to good mood
c. content is to bad mood
d. frustrated is to good mood

11. sweater is to **attire** as
a. road is to juncture
b. writer is to doctrine
c. scavenger is to jackal
d. bludgeon is to weapon

12. batter is to **stance** as
a. patron is to endowment
b. scavenger is to refuse
c. menial is to drudgery
d. candidate is to position

13. belittle is to **less** as
a. plummet is to more
b. abut is to less
c. encroach is to more
d. convey is to less

14. vulture is to **scavenger** as
a. globe is to explorer
b. orchestra is to conductor
c. goldfish is to aquarium
d. hawk is to predator

15. penal is to **punishment** as
a. judicial is to justice
b. stoical is to education
c. liable is to impunity
d. fervent is to apathy

16. defile is to **purify** as
a. capitulate is to give up
b. waver is to stand fast
c. nullify is to make clear
d. proclaim is to hold out

17. edible is to **eaten** as
a. manual is to automated
b. perceptible is to seen
c. tangible is to sensed
d. visual is to blinded

18. spy is to **infiltrate** as
a. sheep is to bleat
b. pig is to wallow
c. mole is to tunnel
d. horse is to trot

Identification   *In each of the following groups, encircle the word that is best defined or suggested by the introductory phrase.*

1. has a way of making other people feel unimportant
a. nullify   b. belittle   c. parry   d. fend

2. with her hat twisted to one side
a. awry   b. encroached   c. chafed   d. predatory

3. the kind of person who doesn't "put up a big front"
a. unassuming   b. dire   c. menial   d. abutting

4. looks for items in junk piles
a. crony   b. proxy   c. scavenger   d. mien

5. like Mozart, who wrote his first opera at the age of nine
a. prodigy   b. enmity   c. attribute   d. stance

6. the point at which the head and the neck meet
a. renown   b. acme   c. juncture   d. bludgeon

7. gave my lawyer the right to act for me
a. enmity   b. menial   c. attribute   d. proxy

8. a change that everyone noticed
a. perceptible   b. exotic   c. predominant   d. predatory

9. make use of strong arguments to overcome all objections
a. abut   b. bludgeon   c. encroach   d. endow

10. cause constant irritation or bitterness
a. endow   b. capitulate   c. rankle   d. convey

11. so pleasant that we couldn't be angry with him
a. gaunt   b. disarming   c. jaunty   d. tawdry

12. a remark that can be interpreted in several different ways
a. cryptic   b. unflagging   c. exotic   d. unassuming

13. an amazing ability to get away with anything
a. renown   b. impunity   c. prodigy   d. stint

14. a lion hunting a wildebeest on the African plain
a. unassuming   b. predatory   c. disgruntled   d. divergent

15. a nagging feeling that they had taken advantage of me
a. stoical   b. disgruntled   c. fervent   d. dire

16. will join any side that he thinks is going to win
a. recluse   b. bludgeon   c. infiltration   d. turncoat

17. made all our efforts completely useless
a. stinted   b. chafed   c. defiled   d. nullified

18. has no respect for the privacy of others
a. capitulate   b. encroach   c. waver   d. rankle

19. an important new idea in our foreign policy
a. doctrine   b. wallow   c. attribute   d. enmity

20. announce to all the people in the world
a. attire   b. convey   c. excise   d. proclaim

Shades of Meaning — *Read each sentence carefully. Then encircle the item that best completes the statement below the sentence.*

In an upper-class Victorian kitchen both the cooks and the menials who assisted them were usually under the direct authority of the housekeeper. **(2)**

1. The word **menials** in line 1 may best be defined as
a. field hands
b. scullions
c. domestic staff
d. parlormaids

To shield their sensitive skin from sunburn, hippopotamuses will often use an old streambed as a wallow in which to coat themselves with a protective layer of mud. **(2)**

2. In line 2 the word **wallow** most nearly means
a. place to eat
b. place to roll
c. place to rest
d. place to sleep

Academic freedom guarantees that all views—both the conventional and the divergent—will be given a fair hearing free of outside interference. **(2)**

3. The best definition for the words **the divergent** in line 2 is
a. those departing from the normal
b. those that are mistaken
c. those going off in different directions
d. those differing from each other

"Although my distinguished colleague's research clearly abuts my own," the famous archaeologist replied, "the conclusions we have drawn are very different." **(2)**

4. In line 1 the word **abuts** most nearly means
a. supports
b. leans against
c. connects with
d. borders on

As soon as our regulars in their scarlet jackets began to defile through the pass, the hill tribesmen of the area opened fire on them from the heights above. **(2)**

5. The best definition for **defile** in line 1 is
a. double-time it
b. straggle
c. thread their way
d. proceed

Antonyms — *In each of the following groups, encircle the word or expression that is most nearly the **opposite** of the first word in **boldface type**.*

1. jaunty
a. ugly
b. gloomy
c. loud
d. thin

2. fervent
a. near
b. cool
c. lowly
d. fresh

3. impunity
a. bigness
b. praise
c. acceptance
d. liability

4. exotic
a. clumsy
b. agreeable
c. familiar
d. stately

5. renown
a. danger
b. newness
c. obscurity
d. justice

6. haggard
a. secret
b. rosy-cheeked
c. sweet
d. kind

7. enmity
a. bottom
b. love
c. belief
d. top

8. chafe
a. fight
b. announce
c. relax
d. soothe

9. stoical
a. close
b. excitable
c. neighboring
d. hidden

10. excise
a. take out
b. hold up
c. go under
d. put in

11. predominant
a. strong
b. severe
c. secondary
d. crooked

12. unassuming
a. worn
b. arrogant
c. happy
d. steady

13. awry
a. lopsided
b. curved
c. straight
d. upside-down

14. perceptible
a. unprepared
b. unmerciful
c. unnoticeable
d. unintentional

15. belittle
a. hire
b. lower
c. enjoy
d. exaggerate

16. pertinent
a. tired
b. unrelated
c. abolished
d. quiet

17. gaunt
a. tired
b. friendly
c. wasteful
d. fat

18. plummet
a. rise
b. fall
c. find
d. free

19. stint
a. employ
b. attempt
c. squander
d. reveal

20. defile
a. scatter
b. obey
c. hide
d. purify

Completing the Sentence

From the following words, choose the one that best completes each of the sentences below. Write the word in the appropriate space.

Group A

waver	proclaim	avail	nullify
rankle	pertinent	scavenger	recluse
crony	perceptible	abut	apt

1. Because their team was so much taller, all our efforts to get the rebounds were of no _____ .

2. In the last years of his life, having lost all desire for human company, he became a(n) _____ .

3. I hereby _____ to all friends and acquaintances, old and new, that I don't want to be asked where I got my red hair.

4. It seems to be typical of human nature that we are all _____ to believe what we want to believe.

5. Though our line _____ under the force of the enemy's attack, it did not buckle.

Group B

dire	mien	defile	proxy
capitulate	stint	plummet	infiltrate
attire	cryptic	stance	convey

1. His gloomy _____ told me as clearly as words that he had lost the tennis match.

2. Unfortunately, on more than one occasion the claim that enemy agents had _____ our security agencies has proven all too true.

3. Although they are far from rich, they will not _____ on anything that they believe is really important for their children.

4. It is certainly to the Senator's credit that she was willing to change her _____ on the issue when we brought new facts to her attention.

5. The message the telephone operator left me was so _____ that I wasn't even sure who had called.

Word Families

A. *On the line provided, write a* **noun form** *of each of the following words.*

EXAMPLE: predominant — **predominance**

1. proclaim   _____

2. apt   _____

3. encroach   _____

4. capitulate   _____

5. convey   _____

6. penal   _____

7. fervent   _____

8. disgruntled   _____

9. nullify   _____

10. predatory   _____

11. tawdry   _____

12. stoical   _____

13. abut   _____

B. *On the line provided, write a* **verb form** *of each of the following words.*

EXAMPLE: penal — **penalize**

1. attribution   _____

2. encroachment   _____

3. predominant   _____

4. doctrine   _____

5. null   _____

6. divergent   _____

7. available   _____

8. excision   _____

9. disarming   _____

10. scavenger   _____

R

Filling the Blanks

Encircle the pair of words that best complete the meaning of each of the following sets of sentences.

1. At first, I was perfectly content to do the rather _____ tasks that my summer job involved. But as time went on, I became thoroughly _____ with such undemanding and oftentimes unpleasant assignments.
   a. exotic . . . obsessed
   b. unassuming . . . endowed
   c. menial . . . disgruntled
   d. tawdry . . . intrigued

2. For a while the politician stood high in public favor, but then his reputation suddenly _____ to earth. One day he was basking in the sunshine of popular approval; the next he found himself _____ under the yoke of universal disfavor.
   a. plummeted . . . chafing
   b. wavered . . . encroaching
   c. parried . . . wallowing
   d. belittled . . . rankling

3. The old adage that "Clothes often _____ the man" simply means that a person's _____ is frequently a kind of public statement about his or her personality.
   a. convey . . . renown
   b. attribute . . . mien
   c. defile . . . stance
   d. proclaim . . . attire

4. A dreadful disease had reduced my friend to a pale shadow of her former self. For that reason, I did not at first recognize the _____ figure that lay in the bed before me. Indeed, it took me some time to find the happy, carefree girl that I had known in the drawn and _____ face that I was looking at.
   a. cryptic . . . jaunty
   b. ravaged . . . disarming
   c. gaunt . . . haggard
   d. stinted . . . fervent

5. Though they never seem to think alike on any subject, there isn't even the slightest hint of _____ between them. I find that somewhat surprising. Usually two people whose views _____ so sharply dislike one another intensely.
   a. juncture . . . abut
   b. enmity . . . diverge
   c. impunity . . . encroach
   d. doctrine . . . nullify

6. During the deciding game, the challenger, a 12-year-old _____ by the name of Mikie, _____ the moves of the champion, herself a grand master and noted chess authority, with all the skill and expertise of an accomplished veteran.
   a. prodigy . . . parried
   b. crony . . . belittled
   c. recluse . . . nullified
   d. acme . . . fended off

Analogies   *In each of the following, encircle the letter of the item that best completes the comparison.*

1. task is to **menial** as
a. appearance is to frugal
b. attitude is to servile
c. mien is to jaunty
d. mood is to haggard

2. belittle is to **minimize** as
a. nullify is to invalidate
b. abut is to encroach
c. venerate is to deplore
d. attire is to undress

3. fervent is to **enthusiasm** as
a. smug is to discontent
b. unassuming is to pride
c. blasé is to boredom
d. clumsy is to finesse

4. resolute is to **waver** as
a. frivolous is to banter
b. prodigal is to stint
c. skittish is to cower
d. solicitous is to veer

5. nonenity is to **renown** as
a. laggard is to perspective
b. recluse is to emotion
c. prodigy is to finesse
d. plebeian is to status

6. awry is to **straight** as
a. oblique is to direct
b. wanton is to bent
c. gaunt is to crooked
d. devoid is to level

7. disgruntled is to **satisfaction** as
a. aghast is to horror
b. abashed is to composure
c. audacious is to courage
d. articulate is to premonition

8. perceptible is to **notice** as
a. unflagging is to waver
b. enterprising is to venture
c. plausible is to doubt
d. audible is to hear

9. relevant is to **pertinent** as
a. volatile is to explosive
b. penal is to painful
c. staid is to tawdry
d. predominant is to menial

10. distraught is to **anguish** as
a. predatory is to impunity
b. stoical is to enmity
c. ethical is to longevity
d. haughty is to disdain

Shades of Meaning   *Read each sentence carefully. Then encircle the item that best completes the statement below the sentence.*

Under the year 1229 it is recorded that Henry III conveyed the earldom of Leicester to his faithful retainer Simon de Montfort by deed of gift.   **(2)**

1. In line 1 the word **conveyed** most nearly means
a. communicated
b. transported
c. imported
d. transferred

As I stepped from the plane, I noticed that the great metropolis was once again attired in its gloomy blanket of fog.   **(2)**

2. The best meaning for **attired** in line 2 is
a. shimmering   b. spruced up   c. draped   d. decked out

On that fervent day in the desert the temperature rose to 120°F, and every particle of sand seemed to glow like a hot coal underfoot.   **(2)**

3. The word **fervent** in line 1 can best be defined as
a. enthusiastic   b. scorching   c. passionate   d. flaming

So Scrooge concludes, while in the corner poor Bob Cratchit chafes his
hands in a furious attempt to keep some semblance of the divine spark
alive in him. **(2)**

4. In line 1 the word **chafes** most nearly means
   a. irritates   c. rubs
   b. torments   d. claps

"And just who is that elegant incognito dancing with the marquise?" Claudia
inquired casually of Lestat as they sauntered through the Palais-Royal. **(2)**

5. The most satisfactory definition for **incognito** in line 1 is
   a. masker   c. celebrity
   b. hermit   d. dancer

**Filling
the Blanks**   *Encircle the pair of words that best complete the
meaning of each of the following sentences.*

1. On almost any day of the week, "Pops" Rafferty can be found at the local
   social club swapping wisecracks with one of his _____ or
   engaging in a bit of good-natured _____ with a perfect
   stranger.
   a. proxies . . . doctrine   c. cronies . . . banter
   b. recluses . . . wrangling   d. apparitions . . . intrigue

2. During that unusual winter warm spell, temperatures _____
   for days around the 70-degree mark, but they _____ to
   record-breaking lows when the next cold front passed through.
   a. hovered . . . plummeted   c. mustered . . . wallowed
   b. basked . . . jostled   d. evolved . . . reverted

3. Even though he had _____ a series of crushing defeats,
   King Alfred steadfastly refused to _____ to the apparently
   unbeatable enemy.
   a. parried . . . incapacitate   c. instilled . . . rehabilitate
   b. proclaimed . . . pulverize   d. sustained . . . capitulate

4. The tornado had _____ the area with such devasting effect
   that in places whole towns had been reduced to nothing more than piles of
   twisted _____ .
   a. precluded . . . residue   c. ravaged . . . rubble
   b. incapacitated . . . detriment d. maimed . . . glut

5. "Like an indulgent parent, Nature has been truly _____ in
   the gifts with which she has _____ this part of the country,"
   I observed.
   a. indiscriminate . . . infiltrated c. wanton . . . stinted
   b. bountiful . . . endowed   d. staid . . . allotted

Unit 10

Definitions

Note carefully the spelling, pronunciation, and definition of each of the following words. Then write the word in the space in the illustrative phrase following.

1. accord
(ə 'kôrd)

(*n.*) agreement, harmony; (*v.*) to agree, be in harmony or bring into harmony; to grant, bestow on

reach an _____

2. barter
('bär tər)

(*n.*) an exchange in trade; (*v.*) to exchange goods

to _____ grain for oil

3. curt
(kərt)

(*adj.*) short, rudely brief

hurt by her _____ reply

4. devise
(di 'vīz)

(*v.*) to think out, plan, figure out, invent, create

_____ a foolproof scheme

5. dexterous
('dek strəs)

(*adj.*) skillful in the use of hands or body; clever

a great dancer's _____ movements

6. engross
(en 'grōs)

(*v.*) to occupy the complete attention, absorb fully

completely _____ in the project

7. entail
(*v.*, en 'tāl;
n., 'en tāl)

(*v.*) to put a burden on, impose, require, involve; to restrict (ownership of property) by limiting inheritance; (*n.*) such a restriction

_____ great expense to the owners

8. ferret
('fer ət)

(*n.*) a kind of a weasel; (*v.*) to search or hunt out; to torment, badger

_____ out the truth

9. habituate
(hə 'bich ü āt)

(*v.*) to become used to; to cause to become used to

_____ to strict discipline

10. impending
(im 'pen diŋ)

(*adj., part.*) about to happen, hanging over (in a menacing way)

signs of _____ danger

11. personable
('pərs nə bəl)

(*adj.*) pleasing in appearance or personality, attractive

a _____ receptionist

12. rue
(rü)

(*v.*) to regret, be sorry for; (*n.*) a feeling of regret

_____ his lost opportunity

13. scoff
(skäf)

(*v.*) to make fun of; to show contempt for

_____ at their ridiculous story

14. transition
(tran 'zish ən)

(*n.*) a change from one state or condition

a city in _____

15. trepidation
(trep ə 'dā shən)

(*n.*) fear, fright, trembling

approached his new school with _____

77

10

16. **upbraid**
(əp ′brād)

(v.) to blame, scold, find fault with

_____ her for her carelessness

17. **veritable**
(′ver ə tə bəl)

(adj.) actual, true, real

prove to be a _____ treasure

18. **vex**
(veks)

(v.) to annoy, anger, exasperate; to confuse, baffle

_____ by their teasing

19. **vitality**
(vī ′tal ə tē)

(n.) strength, energy, liveliness; the capacity to live and develop; the power to endure or survive

enjoying the _____ of youth

20. **whimsical**
(′whim zə kəl)

(adj.) subject to odd ideas, notions, or fancies, playful; unpredictable

a _____ account of her trip

Completing the Sentence

From the words for this unit, choose the one that best completes each of the following sentences. Write the word in the space provided.

1. When I think of all the things that may go wrong, I view the job ahead with great _____ .

2. Since she seems to have known everyone of importance in her time, her diaries read like a(n) _____ Who's Who of the period.

3. Although I have read *Peter Pan* many times, the _____ characters and imaginative story never fail to amuse me.

4. I don't expect long explanations, but why must his answers to my questions be so _____ ?

5. Her early years on a family farm _____ her to long hours and hard manual labor.

6. During those difficult years the state was in the hands of a "do-nothing" administration completely lacking in _____ and direction.

7. A well-known theater in Virginia that accepts various kinds of food as the price of admission is called the "_____ Theater."

8. Before applying for that job, you should know that it _____ the use of a computer.

9. The purpose of this meeting is to _____ a plan for dealing with air pollution in our community.

10. Although the salesperson didn't seem to know the stock very well, she was so pleasant and _____ that we were very glad to have her serving us.

11. We disagree about most things, but we are in perfect _____ in not wanting Aunt Emma as the chaperon at the party.

12. You should not allow yourself to become so _____ by petty annoyances.

13. Every time I go to the dentist, he _____ me for eating things that are bad for my teeth.

14. I assure you that you will _____ the day you challenged Alice to a jogging contest.

15. The _____ fingers of the great violinist were guided by his deep understanding of the music.

16. Throughout most of Africa and Asia, the _____ from colonial status to national independence has been completed.

17. One doesn't have to be a weather specialist to know that the darkening sky is the sign of a(n) _____ storm.

18. For many years she was a highly successful gossip columnist with an extraordinary knack for _____ out the "secrets of the stars."

19. When Ted becomes _____ in a good science-fiction story, he seems completely unaware of everything around him.

20. Before you make fun of my new automatic back scratcher, remember how people _____ at Edison and the Wright brothers.

21. The firefighters who made that daring rescue from a burning building fully deserve all the honors _____ them.

Synonyms   *From the words for this unit, choose the one that is most nearly **the same** in meaning as each of the following groups of expressions. Write the word on the line given.*

1. dread, anxiety, apprehension   _____

2. changeover, conversion, switch, passage   _____

3. attractive, charming, agreeable, likable   _____

4. to regret, lament, repent   _____

5. odd, peculiar, quaint; fanciful, playful   _____

6. about to happen, imminent, upcoming   _____

7. energy, vigor, stamina; liveliness   _____

8. to involve, require, necessitate   _____

9. to track down, hunt out, sniff out   _____

10. skillful, agile, handy, deft   _____

11. to irritate, annoy, irk; to puzzle _____

12. to ridicule, laugh at, jeer at _____

13. to trade, exchange, swap _____

14. to scold, bawl out, reprimand _____

15. rude, brusque, terse, summary _____

16. true, actual _____

17. agreement, mutual understanding _____

18. to get used to, acclimate, inure _____

19. to absorb, immerse, preoccupy _____

20. to concoct, contrive, work out, design _____

Antonyms *From the words for this unit, choose the one that is most nearly **opposite** in meaning to each of the following groups of expressions. Write the word on the line given.*

1. to have no regrets, be thankful for, cherish _____

2. confidence, self-assurance, poise _____

3. to please, delight; to soothe, mollify _____

4. distant, remote _____

5. serious, sober, matter-of-fact, realistic _____

6. false, specious _____

7. clumsy, awkward, ungainly _____

8. to praise, pat on the back _____

9. to take seriously; to admire, revere _____

10. disagreement, conflict, friction _____

11. to bore, put to sleep, stultify _____

12. civil, courteous; lengthy, detailed _____

13. lifelessness, torpor, lethargy _____

14. unpleasant, disagreeable, obnoxious _____

15. to sell; to buy, purchase _____

16. to deprogram, brainwash _____

17. to exclude, rule out, preclude _____

Choosing the *Encircle the **boldface** word that more satisfactorily*
Right Word *completes each of the following sentences.*

1. The years of adolescence mark the (**transition, accord**) from childhood to adulthood.

2. During the oil crisis, Americans became (**habituated, vexed**) to lower temperatures indoors and a decreased use of private cars.

3. She is full of (**veritable, whimsical**) ideas that may not be practical but are a lot of fun to talk over.

4. The telegram contained a(n) (**impending, curt**) message ordering me to return home as soon as possible.

5. In spite of my (**transition, trepidation**) before I made the talk to the assembly, I actually found it a rather enjoyable experience.

6. A long series of minor illnesses sapped his (**vitality, transition**), leaving him unable to work.

7. Instead of trying to (**rue, devise**) an elaborate excuse, why not tell them frankly just what happened and hope for the best?

8. When we moved from an apartment to a house, we found that being a homeowner (**entails, scoffs**) more responsibilities than we had imagined.

9. "And fools who came to (**scoff, ferret**) remained to pray."

10. Millions of people, not only in India but in all parts of the world, came to regard Gandhi as a (**veritable, dexterous**) saint.

11. I must admit that we deserved to be (**engrossed, upbraided**) for failing to follow the safety precautions in the science lab.

12. My uncle told me that dropping out of school at an early age was a decision he has always (**rued, ferreted**).

13. I wouldn't describe Marianne as just (**personable, veritable**)—she is a truly captivating woman.

14. The President needs capable assistants who will shield him from being (**vexed, devised**) by minor problems.

15. Despite my best efforts, I was unable to (**habituate, ferret**) out the time and place of the surprise party.

16. The mayor spoke of (**engrossing, impending**) disaster unless measures were taken immediately to conserve the water supply.

17. Although we all long for world peace, we should not allow ourselves to (**barter, devise**) away our liberties to secure it.

18. The study of irregular verbs may not be too (**engrossing, upbraiding**), but you'll have to master them if you want to learn French.

19. We are attending the meeting in the hope that we will be able to work out some kind of (**accord, trepidation**) on limiting nuclear weapons.

20. Good office managers use their powers so (**dexterously, curtly**) that they accomplish what they want with the least possible upset to everyone.

Unit 11

Definitions

Note carefully the spelling, pronunciation, and definition of each of the following words. Then write the word in the blank space in the illustrative phrase following.

1. appease
(ə 'pēz)

(*v.*) to make calm, soothe; to relieve, satisfy; to yield to

food to _____ their hunger

2. belated
(bi 'lā tid)

(*adj.*) late, tardy

a _____ arrival

3. calamitous
(kə 'lam it əs)

(*adj.*) causing great misfortune

a _____ earthquake

4. cite
(sīt)

(*v.*) to quote; to mention; to summon to appear in court; to commend, recommend

_____ as an authority

5. conventional
(kən 'ven shə nəl)

(*adj.*) in line with accepted ideas or standards; trite

had rather _____ tastes in clothing

6. decoy
(*v.*, di 'koi;
n., 'dē koi)

(*v.*) to lure into a trap; (*n.*) a person or thing used to lure into a trap

used a wooden duck as a _____

7. delve
(delv)

(*v.*) to dig; to search deeply and thoroughly in

_____ into the causes of inflation

8. ensue
(en 'sü)

(*v.*) to follow in order, come immediately after and as a result

regardless of what may _____

9. gallantry
('gal ən trē)

(*n.*) heroic courage; respect and courtesy; an act or statement marked by a high level of courtesy

a display of true _____

10. impart
(im 'pärt)

(*v.*) to make known, tell; to give, pass something on

_____ knowledge to others

11. judicious
(jü 'dish əs)

(*adj.*) using or showing good judgment, wise, sensible

reach a _____ decision

12. mediate
(*v.*, 'mē dē āt;
adj., 'mē dē ət)

(*v.*) to bring about an agreement between persons or groups, act as a go-between; (*adj.*) occupying a middle position; indirect, acting through an intermediary

_____ the dispute

13. milieu
(mēl 'yù)

(*n.*) the setting, surroundings, environment

coming from a different _____

14. outlandish
(aut 'land ish)

(*adj.*) strange, freakish, odd, foreign-looking; geographically remote; exceeding reasonable limits

shocked by his _____ costume

15. overbearing
(o vər 'bâr iŋ)

(adj.) domineering, haughty, bullying; overpowering, predominant

disliked the _____ office manager

16. pert
(pərt)

(adj.) high-spirited; lively; bold, saucy; jaunty

given to making _____ remarks

17. quirk
(kwərk)

(n.) a peculiar way of acting; a sudden twist or turn

a person full of odd _____

18. regale
(ri 'gāl)

(v.) to feast, entertain agreeably

_____ them with stories

19. shiftless
('shift ləs)

(adj.) lazy, lacking in ambition and energy; inefficient

will not hire such a _____ person

20. taint
(tānt)

(n.) a stain or spot; a mark of corruption or dishonor;
(v.) to stain or contaminate

felt that the evidence was _____

**Completing
the Sentence**

From the words for this unit, choose the one that best completes each of the following sentences. Write the word in the space provided.

1. His devil-may-care attitude toward his job eventually earned him quite a

reputation for being _____ and unreliable.

2. As my friend became older, the _____ in his behavior grew
stranger and more difficult to live with.

3. After 50 years of public service, he has a splendid record without the

slightest _____ of wrongdoing.

4. After my bitter quarrel with my brother, he tried to _____ me
by offering to lend me his bicycle.

5. After seven owners had made additions to the house, all in different styles,

the building looked so _____ that no one would buy it.

6. Having grown up in a(n) _____ where children were
supposed to be "seen and not heard," my grandfather finds it hard to
understand the more outspoken behavior of young people today.

7. In spite of all that has been reported about pollution, some people

still do not grasp its _____ effects on the environment.

8. "In that smart new outfit, you look as _____ and appealing
as a schoolgirl," I said to Mother.

9. Although I know I should have written long before now, will you please

accept my _____ thanks for the beautiful gift you sent me.

10. Giving up your bus seat to a pretty girl is showing off, but giving it up to a tired old lady is true _____ .

11. A good teacher can give you knowledge and skills, but no teacher can _____ the wisdom that comes only with experience.

12. We all know that Coach Wohl is strict, but can you _____ a single instance in which she was unfair?

13. Without trying to _____ deeply into the reasons for their conduct, just describe accurately what they did.

14. Marty is one of those people who will never do the _____ thing when it is possible to behave in an unusual or shocking way.

15. A good supervisor is one who can be firm and efficient without giving the impression of being _____ .

16. He _____ us with food, drink, and endless stories of his seafaring days.

17. When we were excited and confused, it was only her _____ advice that prevented us from doing something foolish.

18. When the American people learned of the bombing of Pearl Harbor in December, 1941, they realized that war must _____ .

19. I don't like listening to two people quarrel, but I like even less being the person to _____ their disagreements.

20. Two of the youngsters acted as _____ , while a third tried to swipe a few apples from the unguarded bin.

21. We could not drink from our well because chemical wastes had somehow seeped in and _____ the water.

22. When the witness on the stand proved uncooperative, the judge promptly _____ him for contempt of court.

Synonyms   *From the words for this unit, choose the one that is most nearly **the same** in meaning as each of the following groups of expressions. Write the word on the line given.*

1. the setting, environment, surroundings   _____

2. lively, vivacious; saucy, impudent, fresh   _____

3. peculiar, weird, bizarre; unorthodox, unconventional; out-of-the-way   _____

4. careless, sloppy, lackadaisical   _____

5. high-handed, domineering; overriding   _____

6. chivalrousness; valor, daring   _____

7. to stain, soil, tarnish, pollute; a blot   _____

84

8. to settle, arbitrate, umpire, referee   _____

9. to follow, come after, result   _____

10. to entertain, amuse, divert   _____

11. a peculiarity, oddity, eccentricity   _____

12. wise, thoughtful, prudent, shrewd, astute   _____

13. to pacify, mollify, placate, propitiate   _____

14. to pass on, transmit; to bestow, grant   _____

15. ordinary, commonplace, orthodox   _____

16. to lure, entice, entrap; a lure, bait   _____

17. to refer to, enumerate; to subpoena   _____

18. tardy, delayed, behindhand   _____

19. to dig into, probe, investigate   _____

20. disastrous, catastrophic, ruinous, fatal   _____

Antonyms   From the words for this unit, choose the one that is most nearly **the opposite** in meaning to each of the following groups of expressions. Write the word on the line given.

1. foolish, thoughtless, ill-considered   _____

2. meek, unassuming, self-effacing   _____

3. to withhold, keep back, conceal   _____

4. to purify, decontaminate, cleanse   _____

5. to precede, come before   _____

6. early, ahead of time   _____

7. to enrage, provoke, irritate   _____

8. cowardice; boorishness   _____

9. to ignore, disregard, make no mention of   _____

10. fortunate, beneficial, salutary   _____

11. outlandish, bizarre, unorthodox   _____

12. sullen, gloomy, morose, peevish   _____

13. conventional, orthodox; staid, sober   _____

14. energetic, hardworking, ambitious   _____

Choosing the Right Word   *Encircle the* **boldface** *word that more satisfactorily completes each of the following sentences.*

1. Helen came in this morning to (**regale, delve**) us with all the gossip we had missed during our two-week trip.

2. The company had called in an efficiency expert to increase productivity and root out (**judicious, shiftless**) work habits.

3. Language that seems appropriate in the (**milieu, taint**) of the locker room may be totally out of place in the classroom.

4. We will not allow ourselves to be (**decoyed, imparted**) into supporting candidates who try to mislead the voters.

5. Though Benedict Arnold originally fought for the American cause, his name is forever (**tainted, ensued**) by his ultimate act of treachery.

6. In debate he has the (**overbearing, shiftless**) manner of one who believes firmly that he is never wrong.

7. The best way to (**regale, impart**) a spirit of patriotism to young people is to make them understand the ideals on which this nation is built.

8. Foolishly, Neville Chamberlain attempted to avoid a second world war by (**citing, appeasing**) Hitler's demands for territory in Europe.

9. I am taking this step with my eyes open, and I will accept full responsibility for whatever may (**ensue, impart**).

10. One of the chief functions of the United Nations is to (**appease, mediate**) disagreements between member nations.

11. Instead of relying on a (**judicious, conventional**) textbook, our social studies teacher has us using many different materials and media.

12. The more I (**regale, delve**) into mythology, the more clearly I see how these ancient stories help us understand the basic facts of life.

13. Sue is not a particularly pretty girl, but her high spirits and (**overbearing, pert**) personality make her very attractive.

14. When he finally made his (**belated, judicious**) repayment of the money he owed me, he acted as though he were doing me a big favor.

15. Though some people believe that we should make more use of nuclear power, others insist that such a decision would be (**calamitous, judicious**).

16. If you can believe a story as (**outlandish, conventional**) as that, I think you can believe anything!

17. Whatever his later failures, let us remember that he won the nation's highest military decoration for (**gallantry, milieu**) in action.

18. As every baseball player knows, a knuckleball is extremely hard to hit because its flight is full of unexpected (**quirks, milieus**) called "breaks."

19. By careful planning and (**shiftless, judicious**) investments, he increased greatly the fortune his parents had left him.

20. Although some may call such happenings silly "fairy tales," I can (**cite, appease**) many true instances of poor boys who became President.

Unit 12

Note carefully the spelling, pronunciation, and definition of each of the following words. Then write the word in the blank space in the illustrative phrase following.

1. abdicate
('ab də kāt)

(v.) to resign, formally give up an office or a duty; to disown, discard

forced to _____ the throne

2. bestow
(bi 'stō)

(v.) to give as a gift; to provide with lodgings

_____ honors on the hero

3. capacious
(kə 'pā shəs)

(adj.) able to hold much, roomy

coveralls with _____ pockets

4. caustic
('kô stik)

(adj.) able to burn or eat away by chemical action; biting, sarcastic

a _____ substance like potash

5. crusade
(krü 'sād)

(n.) a strong movement to advance a cause or idea; (v.) to campaign, work vigorously

a _____ against pollution

6. deface
(di 'fās)

(v.) to injure or destroy the surface or appearance of; to damage the value, influence, or effect of; to face down, outshine

_____ a wall by scribbling on it

7. embargo
(em 'bär gō)

(n.) an order forbidding the trade in or movement of commercial goods; any restraint or hindrance; (v.) to forbid to enter or leave port; to forbid trade with

a grain _____

8. fallacy
('fal ə sē)

(n.) a false notion or belief; an error in thinking

a conclusion based on a _____

9. levity
('lev ə tē)

(n.) a lack of seriousness or earnestness, especially about things that should be treated with respect; buoyancy, lightness in weight

discourage _____

10. mendicant
('men də kənt)

(n.) a beggar; (adj.) depending on begging for a living

many _____ pleading for handouts

11. nauseate
('nô zē āt)

(v.) to make sick to the stomach; to fill with disgust

_____ us by his selfishness

12. negate
(ni 'gāt)

(v.) to nullify, deny, bring to nothing

_____ everything I have stood for

13. pivotal
('piv ət əl)

(adj.) vitally important, essential

the _____ issue of the debate

14. recipient
(ri 'sip ē ənt)

(*n.*) one who receives; (*adj.*) receiving; able or willing to receive

the _____ of a scholarship

15. ruse
(rüz)

(*n.*) an action designed to confuse or mislead, a trick

won by a clever _____

16. teem
(tēm)

(*v.*) to become filled to overflowing; to be present in large quantities

streets _____ with people

17. tenet
('ten ət)

(*n.*) an opinion, belief, or principle held to be true

a _____ of the religion

18. tractable
('trak tə bəl)

(*adj.*) easily managed, easy to deal with; easily wrought, malleable

no trouble with such _____ students

19. ungainly
(ən 'gān lē)

(*adj.*) clumsy, awkward; unwieldy

an _____ package

20. voracious
(vô 'rā shəs)

(*adj.*) having a huge appetite, greedy, ravenous; excessively eager

ate his dinner in a _____ manner

Completing the Sentence

From the words for this unit, choose the one that best completes each of the following sentences. Write the word in the space provided.

1. The horse was often hard to manage, but he was _____ as long as he was headed in the direction of the barn.

2. San Francisco is a city that _____ with color and historic interest.

3. For thousands of years thoughtless tourists have _____ monuments of the past by scratching or carving their initials on them.

4. We observed that although a seal is _____ on land, it is extremely graceful in the water.

5. Though a number of people may be nominated for a particular Oscar each year, usually only one of them is the actual _____ of it.

6. He is such a(n) _____ reader that he often has a book propped up in front of him when he is eating.

7. If any of the _____ material gets on your clothing, wash it off with lukewarm water to prevent it from eating away the fabric.

8. The hard-fought victory over South High was the _____ game of the season because it gave our team the self-confidence it needed to win the championship.

9. Whenever she passed the church, she gave a coin to one of the wretched _____ standing in front of it.

10. Since the Greeks could not capture Troy by force, they resorted to the celebrated _____ of the wooden horse to take the city.

11. The noise in the crowded train station gave me a headache, and the foul odor _____ my stomach.

12. When the Shah of Iran saw that he no longer had the support of the people, he _____ and left the country.

13. His attempts at _____ during the most serious moments of the dedication ceremonies were decidedly out of place.

14. One of the basic _____ of democracy is that all people are equal before the law.

15. Dad said that he liked the fig-banana pie I had invented, but the funny look on his face as he tasted it _____ his words.

16. Don't expect a wealthy old lady to _____ a fortune on you for helping her across the street—particularly if she doesn't want to cross it.

17. The President placed a(n) _____ on the selling of arms to the two nations at war.

18. It was not hard for his critics to shoot holes in his argument because the _____ it contained were as plain as day.

19. Early in this century, reform-minded journalists called "muckrakers" _____ vigorously against corruption in government.

20. I have never seen a car with a trunk _____ enough to hold all the luggage you want to take on any trip!

Synonyms From the words for this unit, choose the one that is most nearly **the same** in meaning as each of the following groups of expressions. Write the word on the line given.

1. a principle, belief, doctrine, precept _____

2. to sicken, disgust _____

3. to mar, disfigure, damage _____

4. giddiness, flippancy, frivolity; fickleness _____

5. submissive, docile, yielding, amenable _____

6. a campaign, organized movement _____

7. to cancel, invalidate, annul, nullify _____

8. a beggar, panhandler _____

9. a stoppage, ban, boycott _____

10. a trick, stratagem, subterfuge, dodge _____

11. a false notion, misconception, error _____

12. gluttonous, ravenous, insatiable; avid _____

13. to give, grant, confer; to lodge, put up _____

14. burning, corrosive; sharp, sarcastic _____

15. crucial, critical, decisive, seminal _____

16. roomy, spacious, commodious _____

17. a receiver, beneficiary _____

18. to step down, resign, relinquish, renounce _____

19. awkward, clumsy, graceless _____

20. to abound, swarm, overflow _____

Antonyms From the words for this unit, choose the one that is most nearly **opposite** in meaning to each of the following groups of expressions. Write the word on the line given.

1. unimportant, insignificant _____

2. unruly, obstreperous, refractory _____

3. sound reasoning, logic _____

4. to affirm, confirm, corroborate, buttress _____

5. seriousness, humorlessness, solemnity _____

6. nimble, agile, supple, graceful _____

7. a donor, benefactor, contributor _____

8. bland, mild; sugary, saccharine _____

9. to retain, hold on to power or position _____

10. cramped, confined, restricted, narrow _____

11. to be in short supply, be wanting, lack _____

12. to repair, restore, renovate, recondition _____

13. easily satisfied; indifferent, apathetic _____

14. a millionaire; a philanthropist _____

15. to delight, tickle pink _____

16. to receive, take; to take back, take away _____

90

Choosing the Right Word *Encircle the **boldface** word that more satisfactorily completes each of the following sentences.*

1. She has the kind of (**capacious, ungainly**) mind that seems able to hold endless information and ideas on any subject.

2. "All that I have to (**negate, bestow**) on you," said the elderly father to his son, "is an honorable family name."

3. The fact that she is not a member of the Board of Education does not (**negate, abdicate**) her criticisms of the school system.

4. Time and the weather had so (**defaced, nauseated**) the statue that its original expression was no longer distinguishable.

5. A favorite bedtime (**ruse, bestow**) of small children is to keep asking for a glass of water to delay having to go to sleep.

6. It's good to be open to new ideas, but don't try to become so (**mendicant, tractable**) that you have no firm opinions of your own.

7. One guiding (**levity, tenet**) of our energy program is that it is just as important to avoid wasting energy as to increase its production.

8. The tall boy who appeared so (**ungainly, pivotal**) as he walked through the school corridors was graceful and coordinated on the basketball court.

9. Has anyone ever measured how many hours of TV time are needed to satisfy a small child's (**voracious, tractable**) appetite for cartoons?

10. We will not allow you to (**nauseate, abdicate**) your responsibilities as a leading citizen of this community.

11. Isn't it a (**fallacy, tenet**) to say that because no woman has ever been elected President, no woman is qualified to serve in that office?

12. She is a very severe critic, and the (**capacious, caustic**) comments in her reviews have made her many enemies.

13. When the United States gives out foreign aid, are the (**pivotal, recipient**) nations supposed to make repayment?

14. Although the students made jokes about the coming exams, we knew that beneath the (**levity, ruse**) they were quite worried.

15. Helen's mind is closed, as though she had placed a(n) (**embargo, tenet**) on new information and ideas.

16. Instead of launching a great (**crusade, recipient**) to save the world, why not try to help a few people in your own neighborhood?

17. As soon as the new highway extension was built, the shopping center began to (**teem, negate**) with activity.

18. I can forgive most human weaknesses, but I am (**nauseated, bestowed**) by hypocrisy.

19. I am willing to become a veritable (**mendicant, recipient**) in order to raise money for that most worthy cause.

20. Although the play is named *Julius Caesar*, I think that the (**pivotal, ungainly**) character, on whom all the action depends, is Mark Antony.

Review Units 10–12

Analogies In each of the following, encircle the item that best completes the comparison.

1. ensue is to **after** as
a. precede is to before
b. entail is to after
c. impend is to before
d. engross is to after

2. hero is to **gallantry** as
a. bully is to transition
b. recipient is to vitality
c. mendicant is to levity
d. coward is to trepidation

3. judicious is to **favorable** as
a. capacious is to unfavorable
b. ungainly is to favorable
c. curt is to unfavorable
d. caustic is to favorable

4. disaster is to **calamitous** as
a. ruse is to veritable
b. quirk is to peculiar
c. fallacy is to correct
d. crusade is to pert

5. shovel is to **delve** as
a. cup is to pour
b. water is to boil
c. knife is to cut
d. kitchen is to cook

6. mendicant is to **beg** as
a. recipient is to bestow
b. librarian is to borrow
c. deserter is to crusade
d. host is to regale

7. teeming is to **number** as
a. gigantic is to size
b. overbearing is to manner
c. abundant is to position
d. belated is to time

8. donor is to **bestow** as
a. believer is to scoff
b. teacher is to impart
c. stench is to nauseate
d. thief is to barter

9. juggler is to **dexterous** as
a. coward is to gallant
b. spy is to devious
c. diplomat is to curt
d. banker is to financial

10. ungainly is to **handle** as
a. deaf is to hear
b. tractable is to control
c. veritable is to believe
d. dim is to see

11. mule is to **tractable** as
a. fox is to sly
b. mouse is to meek
c. ox is to intelligent
d. otter is to aquatic

12. king is to **abdicate** as
a. president is to resign
b. author is to cite
c. salesclerk is to barter
d. employee is to dismiss

13. overbearing is to **unfavorable** as
a. personable is to favorable
b. whimsical is to unfavorable
c. shiftless is to favorable
d. tractable is to unfavorable

14. scoff is to **contempt** as
a. engross is to vulgarity
b. mediate is to anger
c. negate is to levity
d. rue is to sorrow

15. milieu is to **setting** as
a. beaver is to ferret
b. accord is to friction
c. tenet is to belief
d. appetite is to voracity

16. hunter is to **decoy** as
a. inventor is to device
b. magician is to ruse
c. policeman is to traffic
d. trader is to embargo

17. personable is to **charm** as
a. overbearing is to wealth
b. judicious is to foolishness
c. pert is to trepidation
d. energetic is to vitality

18. quirk is to **eccentric** as
a. fallacy is to erroneous
b. thimble is to capacious
c. comment is to caustic
d. transition is to impending

Identification   *In each of the following groups, encircle the word that is best defined or suggested by the introductory phrase.*

1. quiet the cranky children by giving them something to eat
a. taint   b. appease   c. delve   d. rue

2. "We view with alarm the rise of crime in this neighborhood."
a. personable   b. gallantry   c. veritable   d. trepidation

3. spring floods following the quick melting of heavy snows
a. ensue   b. entail   c. engross   d. embargo

4. cleverly misled the enemy into thinking we were about to retreat
a. mediate   b. ruse   c. quirk   d. scoff

5. young people full of vim and vigor
a. levity   b. fallacy   c. decoy   d. vitality

6. organized a great national effort to find a cure for cancer
a. trepidation   b. crusade   c. taint   d. accord

7. "Brother, can you spare a dime?"
a. vitality   b. regale   c. mendicant   d. belated

8. like a supertanker or a jumbo jet
a. personable   b. capacious   c. outlandish   d. shiftless

9. the principle of separation of powers in government
a. tenet   b. milieu   c. ungainly   d. recipient

10. constantly cracking your knuckles or pulling your ear
a. taint   b. gallantry   c. quirk   d. ruse

11. final exams coming up next week
a. voracious   b. capacious   c. belated   d. impending

12. the gradual change from a rural to an urban nation
a. transition   b. dexterous   c. taint   d. pivotal

13. reached an agreement on the limitation of nuclear arms
a. embargo   b. accord   c. pert   d. nauseate

14. known for her quiet, sly humor
a. judicious   b. dexterous   c. caustic   d. whimsical

15. a good environment for raising children
a. transition   b. impart   c. milieu   d. cite

16. saucy in a cute, winning way
a. overbearing   b. pert   c. curt   d. tractable

17. like a shark in one's appetites
a. shiftless   b. voracious   c. judicious   d. dexterous

18. cut off trade with certain nations
a. barter   b. devise   c. embargo   d. abdicate

19. "I don't like his sarcastic, critical remarks."
a. conventional   b. calamitous   c. caustic   d. pivotal

20. helped to settle the quarrel between two people
a. mediate   b. negate   c. vex   d. upbraid

Shades of   *Read each sentence carefully. Then encircle the item*
Meaning   *that best completes the statement below the sentence.*

Though the Misses Bennet were indeed their father's daughters, they did
not come into his landed property because, centuries before, inheriting it
had been entailed on the male line.   **(2)**

1. In line 3 the phrase **entailed on** most nearly means
    a. required of   c. restricted to
    b. involved with   d. necessitated by

In Europe the use of the ferret to drive rats and other kinds of vermin out of
their underground burrows has been practiced since Roman times.   **(2)**

2. The best meaning for **ferret** in line 1 is
    a. bird dog   c. badger
    b. weasel   d. nettle

"Time doth transfix the flourish set on youth
And delves the parallels in beauty's brow."
       (Shakespeare, Sonnet 60, 9–10)   **(2)**

3. The word **delves** in line 2 most nearly means
    a. investigates   b. searches out   c. ransacks   d. digs

After the successful defense of Rorke's Drift, eleven members of the
Twenty-Fourth Regiment were cited for gallantry and received the
Victoria Cross.   **(2)**

4. In line 2 the word **cited** is best defined as
    a. commended   b. subpoenaed   c. quoted   d. summoned

"This holy [time] of Christmas
All others doth deface." ("God Rest Ye Merry, Gentlemen")   **(2)**

5. The best meaning for the word **deface** in line 2 is
    a. mar   b. outshine   c. disfigure   d. erase

Antonyms   *In each of the following groups, encircle the word or*
*expression that is most nearly the **opposite** of the first*
*word in **boldface type**.*

1. veritable	**3. abdicate**	**5. taint**	**7. nauseate**
a. cute	a. retain	a. find	a. try
b. false	b. regret	b. attack	b. mislead
c. late	c. scold	c. cleanse	c. please
d. small	d. annoy	d. return	d. begin
2. cite	**4. ungainly**	**6. engross**	**8. vex**
a. oppose	a. odd	a. divide	a. play
b. join	b. serious	b. bore	b. charm
c. hear	c. clean	c. remove	c. give
d. fail to mention	d. graceful	d. depart	d. know

9. appease
a. help
b. provoke
c. start
d. lose

10. negate
a. remove
b. affirm
c. aid
d. deny

11. recipient
a. doubter
b. giver
c. runner
d. seeker

12. trepidation
a. importance
b. confidence
c. end
d. answer

13. tractable
a. clumsy
b. stubborn
c. slow
d. sharp

14. calamitous
a. generous
b. beneficial
c. large
d. tardy

15. judicious
a. careless
b. late
c. simple
d. illegal

16. personable
a. unattractive
b. unreasonable
c. direct
d. beautiful

17. shiftless
a. successful
b. overdressed
c. thoughtful
d. hardworking

18. fallacy
a. success
b. danger
c. truth
d. height

19. caustic
a. sweet
b. secondary
c. unkind
d. slow

20. levity
a. simplicity
b. sarcasm
c. commonness
d. seriousness

Completing the Sentence

From the following words, choose the one that best completes each of the sentences below. Write the word in the appropriate space.

Group A

decoy	trepidation	devise	barter
upbraid	entail	capacious	abdicate
ferret	taint	negate	vitality

1. The coach _____ the team not for losing the game, but for failing to follow his instructions.

2. We will not end this meeting until we have _____ a solution that will satisfy all of us.

3. When we entered the store, we saw that the low price for the camera was only a(n) _____ , and that the prices on other items had not been lowered.

4. A "deadbeat dad" may conveniently be defined as a father who has _____ all responsibility for his offspring.

5. The car is so _____ that the two families and their pets can easily fit in it.

Group B

delve	mediate	vex	nauseate
quirk	regale	habituate	engross
ensue	teem	cite	appease

1. Unfortunately, my attempt to _____ her wrath by proffering the proverbial "olive branch" proved a dismal failure.

2. When you invited me to drop in for a "bite to eat," I certainly didn't expect to be _____ with a feast!

3. During our first few days in the Rockies the thin air felt strange, but by now we have become _____ to it.

4. We chose Ann to _____ the dispute because she doesn't favor either side.

5. During the morning rush hour the streets of every great metropolis _____ with people hurrying to work.

Word Families

A. *On the line provided, write a* **noun form** *of each of the following words.*

EXAMPLE: pivotal — **pivot**

1. calamitous _____
2. abdicate _____
3. nauseate _____
4. negate _____
5. cite _____
6. capacious _____
7. voracious _____
8. whimsical _____
9. bestow _____
10. conventional _____
11. judicious _____
12. dexterous _____

B. *On the line provided, write a* **verb form** *of each of the following words.*

EXAMPLE: rueful — **rue**

1. habitual _____
2. tainted _____
3. vexatious _____
4. nauseous _____
5. entailment _____
6. vitality _____
7. appeasement _____
8. negative _____
9. impending _____
10. recipient _____

**Filling
the Blanks**

*Encircle the pair of words that best complete the
meaning of each of the following sets of sentences.*

1. "My ability to hold on to this job will pretty much depend on the answer to
   one _____ question," I thought. "Will I prove to be truly
   hardworking and reliable, or _____ and irresponsible?"
   a. pivotal . . . shiftless
   b. whimsical . . . personable
   c. impending . . . tractable
   d. caustic . . . dexterous

2. The speaker did not _____ many examples to back up her
   argument, but those that she did provide were extremely well-chosen. A
   larger but less _____ selection of illustrations probably would
   not have made such a powerful impression on the audience.
   a. devise . . . ungainly
   b. impart . . . outlandish
   c. cite . . . judicious
   d. bestow . . . capacious

3. "I certainly don't view the upcoming scholarship examination with any
   _____ ," I asserted confidently. "Still, it's a serious matter,
   and I'm not treating it with undue _____ either."
   a. gallantry . . . vitality
   b. nausea . . . dexterity
   c. curtness . . . vexation
   d. trepidation . . . levity

4. "That rock group's strange antics, _____ costumes, and
   weird songs don't really impress me," Clara remarked. "Frankly, I prefer
   musicians who are much more _____ ."
   a. caustic . . . whimsical
   b. pert . . . overbearing
   c. bartered . . . tainted
   d. outlandish . . . conventional

5. "Though I'd spent all my life in a rural environment, I didn't think I'd have
   any trouble adjusting to city life," Ted said to his friend. "But making the
   _____ to an urban _____ proved to be much
   more difficult than I had imagined."
   a. crusade . . . recipient
   b. tenet . . . embargo
   c. transition . . . milieu
   d. ruse . . . tenet

6. Despite the _____ of a few brave men, whose daring deeds
   on that fateful day are still remembered by history, imperial Rome suffered
   a(n) _____ defeat that brought a once mighty empire to its
   knees.
   a. trepidation . . . veritable
   b. gallantry . . . calamitous
   c. vitality . . . whimsical
   d. dexterity . . . impending

7. Long overdue though it surely was, his _____ apology was
   sufficient to soothe my ruffled feelings and _____ my anger.
   a. belated . . . appease
   b. dexterous . . . vex
   c. curt . . . negate
   d. caustic . . . mediate

Analogies *In each of the following, encircle the letter of the item that best completes the comparison.*

1. **taint** is to **defile** as
a. qualm is to hesitate
b. defect is to repair
c. quirk is to habituate
d. detriment is to harm

2. **scavenger** is to **ferret** as
a. recipient is to endow
b. mendicant is to beg
c. scapegoat is to preclude
d. turncoat is to ravage

3. **willful** is to **tractable** as
a. prone is to apt
b. voracious is to retentive
c. staid is to outlandish
d. whimsical is to frivolous

4. **chain** is to **tether** as
a. ladder is to grope
b. feather is to pulverize
c. spade is to delve
d. screwdriver is to grapple

5. **sequel** is to **ensue** as
a. prologue is to precede
b. preface is to follow
c. aftermath is to introduce
d. finale is to impend

6. **gallantry** is to **audacious** as
a. disdain is to servile
b. enmity is to disgruntled
c. geniality is to aloof
d. wisdom is to judicious

7. **dexterous** is to **finesse** as
a. prodigal is to money
b. pert is to trepidation
c. vivacious is to vitality
d. caustic is to perspective

8. **churlish** is to **personable** as
a. curt is to facetious
b. overbearing is to unassuming
c. conventional is to pivotal
d. belated is to tardy

9. **rue** is to **sorrow** as
a. vex is to enmity
b. upbraid is to plaudits
c. perturb is to antics
d. deplore is to disapproval

10. **shiftless** is to **enterprising** as
a. wavering is to unflagging
b. pertinent is to relevant
c. gingerly is to ungainly
d. ample is to bountiful

11. **capacious** is to **room** as
a. oblique is to direction
b. laggard is to time
c. prodigious is to size
d. jaunty is to attitude

12. **plausible** is to **scoff at** as
a. commendable is to upbraid
b. perceptible is to observe
c. audible is to hear
d. durable is to wear

13. **tenet** is to **doctrine** as
a. banter is to rubble
b. repercussion is to backlash
c. anguish is to intrigue
d. crony is to enemy

14. **wrangle** is to **accord** as
a. ostracize is to favor
b. vie is to rivalry
c. comply is to agreement
d. collaborate is to competition

15. **dire** is to **calamitous** as
a. veritable is to suspect
b. staunch is to resolute
c. cryptic is to intelligent
d. capacious is to congested

16. **blasé** is to **engross** as
a. voracious is to appease
b. wanton is to obsess
c. predatory is to sustain
d. frugal is to amass

17. **country** is to **defect** as
a. job is to oust
b. party is to purge
c. excerpt is to cite
d. throne is to abdicate

18. **entail** is to **preclude** as
a. evolve is to progress
b. assert is to proclaim
c. belittle is to magnify
d. instigate is to provoke

19. inventor is to **devise** as
a. carrier is to convey
b. decoy is to mediate
c. buyer is to barter
d. recluse is to excise

20. fallacy is to **logic** as
a. stance is to baseball
b. solecism is to grammar
c. crusade is to politics
d. jurisdiction is to law

21 eyes are to **peruse** as
a. hooks are to grapple
b. arms are to tether
c. ideas are to instill
d. hands are to grope

22. oblique is to **forthright** as
a. blasé is to frivolous
b. incognito is to avowed
c. discordant is to dissonant
d. congested is to rural

Shades of Meaning

Read each sentence carefully. Then encircle the item that best completes the statement below the sentence.

As Dickens points out, the fierceness with which Mr. Boythorn expresses his opinions hardly accords with his overall mildness of temperament. (2)

1. The best meaning for the phrase **accords with** in line 2 is
a. bestows on
b. approves of
c. adapts to
d. harmonizes with

Once young Mr. Sedley, whose sweet tooth was decidedly pronounced, had glutted himself on chocolates, he fell asleep, much to the annoyance of his sister and Miss Sharp. (2)

2. In line 2 the word **glutted** most nearly means
a. flooded   b. overstuffed   c. choked   d. sickened

As Great Britain pushed its colonial empire to the limit in the late 19th century, English men and women began to turn up in the most inaccessible and outlandish places. (2)

3. The word **outlandish** in line 3 can best be defined as
a. out-of-the-way
b. unconventional
c. freakish
d. foreign-looking

Writing may have come to ancient Egypt directly from Sumer, or it may have arrived by some mediate process involving Syria and Palestine. (2)

4. The best definition of the word **mediate** in line 2 is
a. indirect   b. casual   c. middle   d. agreed

The levity of some gases in respect to air ideally suits them to use in dirigibles, weather balloons, and other such devices. (2)

5. The word **levity** in line 1 most nearly means
a. fickleness   b. lightness   c. frivolity   d. mildness

As soon as it was light, we boarded the old steamer and bestowed ourselves in our berths. (2)

6. The word **bestowed** in line 1 most nearly means
a. amused   b. employed   c. lodged   d. presented

**Filling
the Blanks**

*Encircle the pair of words that best complete the
meaning of each of the following sentences.*

1. Though _____ like the mountain lion and the lynx have
entirely disappeared from the settled parts of this country, they can
still be found in areas that _____ with wildlife.

  a. predators . . . teem
  b. scavengers . . . bask

  c. milieus . . . wallow
  d. decoys . . . cower

2. When labor and management cannot arrive at an agreement through
collective bargaining or some other means, they sometimes have
_____ to outside _____ to settle a dispute.

  a. proximity . . . infiltration
  b. transition . . . intrigue

  c. recourse . . . mediation
  d. proxy . . . jurisdiction

3. With all the fervor of the _____ knights of the Round Table
and other fabled heroes of old, Don Quixote embarked on his hilarious
personal _____ to right the wrongs of the world.

  a. elite . . . embargo
  b. legendary . . . crusade

  c. myriad . . . juncture
  d. renowned . . . ruse

4. Since he derived no pleasure from the more serious pursuits of life, the
fun-loving prince _____ himself with hunts, balls, and other
_____ entertainments.

  a. bolstered . . . solicitous
  b. glutted . . . ethical

  c. regaled . . . frivolous
  d. asserted . . . conventional

5. "Certain misguided students may think that they can _____
school property with _____ , but I assure them that such
acts of vandalism will not go unpunished," the principal warned.

  a. maim . . . longevity
  b. bestow . . . incognito

  c. incapacitate . . . nonentity
  d. deface . . . impunity

6. The presence of a number of people _____ in formal black
evening dress imparted a faint air of elegance and style to the otherwise
_____ surroundings in which the reception was held.

  a. attired . . . tawdry
  b. minimized . . . gaunt

  c. nullified . . . ornate
  d. endowed . . . volatile

7. "The brutal treatment I received from my captors during the war may have
_____ my body, but it has not _____ my
spirit," the ex-POW proudly observed.

  a. incapacitated . . . maimed
  b. invalidated . . . perturbed

  c. congested . . . tethered
  d. jostled . . . precluded

Unit 13

Definitions

Note carefully the spelling, pronunciation, and definition of each of the following words. Then write the word in the blank space in the illustrative phrase following.

1. adapt
(ə 'dapt)

(*v.*) to adjust or change to suit conditions

_____ to a new job

2. attest
(ə 'test)

(*v.*) to bear witness, affirm to be true or genuine

_____ to the truth of her statement

3. dovetail
('dəv tāl)

(*v.*) to fit together exactly; to connect so as to form a whole; (*n.*) a carpentry figure resembling a dove's tail

_____ our activities with theirs

4. enormity
(i 'nôr mə tē)

(*n.*) the quality of exceeding all moral bounds; an exceedingly evil act; huge size, immensity

the _____ of an offense

5. falter
('fôl tər)

(*v.*) to hesitate, stumble, lose courage; to speak hesitatingly; to lose drive, weaken, decline

_____ at the moment of danger

6. foreboding
(fôr 'bō diŋ)

(*n.*) a warning or feeling that something bad will happen; (*adj.*) marked by fear, ominous

filled with _____

7. forlorn
(fôr 'lôrn)

(*adj.*) totally abandoned and helpless; sad and lonely; wretched or pitiful; almost hopeless

the _____ cry of a wolf

8. haughty
('hô tē)

(*adj.*) chillingly proud and scornful

a _____ sneer

9. impediment
(im 'ped ə mənt)

(*n.*) a physical defect; a hindrance, obstacle

an _____ in our path

10. imperative
(im 'per ə tiv)

(*adj.*) necessary, urgent; (*n.*) a form of a verb expressing a command; that which is necessary or required

an _____ message

11. loiter
('loi tər)

(*v.*) to linger in an aimless way, hang around

_____ in the corridors

12. malinger
(mə 'liŋ gər)

(*v.*) to pretend illness to avoid duty or work

accuse of _____

13. pithy
('pith ē)

(*adj.*) short but full of meaning and point

impressed by her _____ explanation

14. plunder
('plən dər)

(*v.*) to rob by force, especially during wartime; to seize wrongfully; (*n.*) property stolen by force, booty

_____ the neighboring farms

15. simper
('sim pər)

(v.) to smile or speak in a silly, forced way; (n.) a silly, forced smile

with a silly _____ on his face

16. steadfast
('sted fast)

(adj.) firmly fixed; constant, not moving or changing

_____ in his desire

17. vaunted
('vônt id)

(adj.) much boasted about in a vain or swaggering way

his _____ courage

18. vilify
('vil ə fī)

(v.) to abuse or belittle unjustly or maliciously

_____ his opponent's reputation

19. waif
(wāf)

(n.) a person (usually a child) without a home or friend; a stray person or animal; something that comes along by chance, a stray bit

pitied the poor _____ on the street

20. wry
(rī)

(adj.) twisted, turned to one side; cleverly and often grimly humorous

responded only with a _____ smile

Completing the Sentence

From the words for this unit, choose the one that best completes each of the following sentences. Write the word in the space provided.

1. He remained _____ in his friendship, even at a time when it might have been to his advantage to have nothing to do with me.

2. The comedian specialized in the kind of _____ humor that gets quiet chuckles from an audience, rather than loud bursts of laughter.

3. The testimony of all the witnesses _____ neatly, forming a strong case against the accused.

4. The quick recovery of the patients _____ to the skill of the hospital staff.

5. The sergeant suspected that the soldiers were _____ in order to avoid dangerous duty.

6. In every great war, many children are separated from their parents and become homeless _____ , begging for food and shelter.

7. When he was caught red-handed in the act of going through my papers, all he did was to stand there and _____ foolishly.

8. When Carole attempted to order the meal in French, we discovered that her much _____ knowledge of that language made no impression at all on the waiter.

9. Through all the shocks and trials of the Civil War, Abraham Lincoln never
_____ in his determination to save the Union.

10. After the official had fallen from power, his policies were ridiculed, his
motives questioned, and his character _____ .

11. The _____ expressions on the faces of the starving children
in the TV special moved the world to pity and indignation at their plight.

12. Her _____ manner said more clearly than words that she
could never associate as an equal with a peasant like me.

13. Great skill is required to _____ a novel or short story for use
as a motion picture.

14. When Jim missed those early foul shots, I had a(n) _____
that the game was going to be a bad one for our team.

15. During our absence, a group of hungry bears broke into the cabin and
_____ our food supply.

16. Now and in the years ahead, it is _____ for us to produce
automobiles that will give us better gas mileage.

17. Please don't _____ in front of the bowling alley because you
will get in the way of people passing by.

18. I appreciate the fact that when I asked her for advice, she gave it to me in
a few clear, direct, and _____ sentences.

19. Unless you take steps now to correct your speech _____ ,
it will be a serious handicap to you throughout your life.

20. The _____ of the crimes that the Nazis committed in the
concentration camps horrified the civilized world.

Synonyms   *From the words for this unit, choose the one that is most
nearly **the same** in meaning as each of the following
groups of expressions. Write the word on the line given.*

1. to hang around, dawdle about, tarry _____

2. loyal, faithful; constant, unwavering _____

3. boasted, trumpeted, heralded _____

4. disdainful, scornful, supercilious _____

5. to pillage, loot, sack; booty, spoils, pelf _____

6. dryly amusing, ironic, droll _____

7. to malign, defame, denigrate, traduce _____

8. essential, indispensable, mandatory _____

9. atrociousness, heinousness; an atrocity;
vastness _____

10. to hesitate, waver, stumble   _____

11. to snicker, smirk, titter, giggle   _____

12. to fit together, mesh, jive, harmonize   _____

13. terse, short and sweet; meaty; telling   _____

14. a misgiving, presentiment, premonition   _____

15. to witness, verify, confirm, corroborate   _____

16. an obstruction, obstacle, stumbling block   _____

17. to regulate, adjust, alter; to acclimate   _____

18. woebegone; forsaken, bereft; pathetic   _____

19. to lie down on the job, goof off, shirk   _____

20. a stray, ragamuffin, street urchin   _____

Antonyms   *From the words for this unit, choose the one that is most nearly* **opposite** *in meaning to each of the following groups of expressions. Write the word on the line given.*

1. inconstant, fickle, unreliable, vacillating   _____

2. to make a beeline for, hurry along   _____

3. meek, humble, unassuming, modest   _____

4. to glorify, extol, lionize   _____

5. nonessential, unnecessary, optional   _____

6. jaunty, buoyant, blithe, chipper   _____

7. to remain unchanged   _____

8. wordy, verbose, long-winded; foolish, inane   _____

9. mildness; harmlessness, innocuousness   _____

10. downplayed, soft-pedaled, de-emphasized   _____

11. humorless, solemn; straight   _____

12. to persevere, plug away at   _____

13. to deny, disprove, refute, rebut   _____

14. a help, advantage, asset, plus   _____

15. a feeling of confidence or optimism   _____

16. to keep one's nose to the grindstone   _____

17. to clash, be at odds, cancel each other out   _____

Choosing the Right Word *Encircle the **boldface** word that more satisfactorily completes each of the following sentences.*

1. We all like the Cinderella story of a poor, mistreated (**waif, malingerer**) who marries a prince and lives happily ever after.

2. Political leaders should feel free to change their minds on specific issues, while remaining (**steadfast, wry**) in their support of their principles.

3. The police sometimes use laws against (**faltering, loitering**) to prevent the gathering of unruly crowds.

4. When she learned that she had not been chosen for the job, she made a (**wry, forlorn**) joke, but this did not conceal her deep disappointment.

5. The advice given by Ben Franklin in *Poor Richard's Almanac* has rarely been equalled for (**pithiness, dovetailing**) and good common sense.

6. Monday morning seems to be a favorite time for practicing the fine art of (**foreboding, malingering**).

7. The temperaments of the partners in the business (**dovetail, attest**) so well that they can work together without the slightest friction or conflict.

8. No matter how well qualified you may be, inability to get on well with other people will prove a serious (**imperative, impediment**) in any field of work.

9. Ample food supplies in the United States (**attest, vilify**) to the abilities of American farmers.

10. In the opening scene of Shakespeare's *Macbeth*, there is a strong sense of (**foreboding, enormity**) that something terrible is going to happen.

11. Mutual respect and understanding among all racial and ethnic groups has become a(n) (**imperative, waif**) in the life of this nation.

12. People who migrate from the suburbs to the inner city often find it difficult to (**adapt, attest**) to changing conditions.

13. The director told Neil to smile like a "dashing man around town," but all he could do was to (**simper, loiter**) like a confused freshman.

14. Thinking it no crime to borrow from the past, Elizabethan dramatists often (**vilified, plundered**) ancient writers for suitable plots for their plays.

15. Despite our own exhaustion, we made one final, (**forlorn, pithy**) attempt to save the drowning swimmer, but our efforts were of no avail.

16. Her (**haughty, steadfast**) attitude toward those she considered "beneath her" was a sure sign of lack of breeding and simple good manners.

17. To (**attest, falter**) now, at the very threshold of victory, would mean that all our earlier struggles and sacrifices had been in vain.

18. Hordes of savage barbarians swept into the province, committing one (**impediment, enormity**) after another on the defenseless population.

19. I can't stand the way he struts and (**loiters, vaunts**) himself in front of girls.

20. "I did what I thought best at the time," the President replied, "and I deeply resent their cowardly attempts to (**vilify, plunder**) my actions."

Unit 14

Definitions Note carefully the spelling, pronunciation, and definition of each of the following words. Then write the word in the blank space in the illustrative phrase following.

1. amplify
('am plə fī)

(v.) to make stronger, larger, greater, louder, or the like

asked him to _____ his statement

2. armistice
('är mə stis)

(n.) a temporary peace, halt in fighting

declare an _____

3. arrogant
('ar ə gənt)

(adj.) haughty, too convinced of one's own importance

criticize him for his _____ attitude

4. bland
(bland)

(adj.) gentle, soothing, mild; lacking interest or taste

a diet of _____ food

5. disclaim
(dis 'klām)

(v.) to deny interest in or connection with; to give up all claim to

_____ membership in the party

6. epoch
('ep ək)

(n.) a distinct period of time, era, age

a memorable _____ in my life

7. estrange
(e 'strānj)

(v.) to drift apart or become unfriendly; to cause such a separation; to remove or keep at a distance

when the brothers became _____

8. gratify
('grat ə fī)

(v.) to please, satisfy; to indulge or humor

_____ their every whim

9. infinite
('in fə nit)

(adj.) exceedingly great, inexhaustible, without limit, endless; (n., preceded by the) an incalculable number, the concept of infinity; (cap. I) a name for God

showed _____ patience

10. irascible
(ir 'as ə bəl)

(adj.) easily made angry, hot-tempered

an _____ boss

11. kindred
('kin drəd)

(n.) a person's relatives; a family relationship; (adj.) related by blood; like, similar

_____ spirits

12. naive
(nä 'ēv)

(adj.) innocent, unsophisticated, showing lack of worldly knowledge and experience

amused by the _____ freshmen

13. niche
(nich)

(n.) a decorative recess in a wall; a suitable place or position for a person or thing

a _____ in the wall

14. obliterate
(ə 'blit ə rāt)

(v.) to blot out completely, destroy utterly

_____ his name from the records

15. ramshackle
('ram shak əl)

(*adj.*) appearing ready to collapse, loose and shaky

the _____ old barn

16. ransack
('ran sak)

(*v.*) to search or examine thoroughly; to rob, plunder

_____ the house for valuables

17. rote
(rōt)

(*n.*) unthinking routine, a fixed or mechanical way of doing something; (*adj.*) based on a mechanical routine

recite his lessons by _____

18. solvent
('säl vənt)

(*adj.*) able to meet one's financial obligations; having the power to dissolve other substances; (*n.*) a liquid used to dissolve other substances; something that solves, explains, eliminates, or softens

a company in a _____ condition

19. tedious
('tē dē əs)

(*adj.*) long and tiresome

a _____ speech

20. vendor
('ven dər)

(*n.*) a person who sells something

the newspaper _____ on the corner

Completing the Sentence

From the words for this unit, choose the one that best completes each of the following sentences. Write the word in the space provided.

1. After four hours of doing the same small task over and over again, I began to find my new job on the assembly line _____ .

2. He used to be a modest, likable fellow, but now that he has come into some money, his manner has become exceedingly _____ and offensive.

3. We did not realize how poor the people in that isolated country were until we saw the _____ huts in which they were living.

4. "Unless we learn to control nuclear weapons," the speaker said, "they may _____ mankind."

5. Although he had been separated from his family for years, in that hour of need all his _____ came to his aid.

6. When the electric power failed, we _____ the kitchen to find candles.

7. "You should understand the reason for all the steps in the problem," our math teacher said, "not simply carry them out by _____ ."

8. We want to buy a component that will _____ the sounds of our hi-fi set without distorting them.

9. Along the walls of the church, there were _____ in which statues of saints had been placed.

10. I think that the vivid phrase "having a short fuse" aptly describes Tom's _____ temperament.

11. "A dinner that is truly well prepared _____ the eye as well as the palate," a famous chef once remarked.

12. How could you have been so _____ and foolish as to take his compliments seriously!

13. I've been broke for so long that I'm afraid I won't know how to behave when I find myself _____ again.

14. After eating those highly spiced foods in Mexico all summer, I found Mother's cooking pleasantly _____ .

15. Increasing dissatisfaction with the direction the party was taking slowly _____ him from it.

16. The tinkling bell of the ice cream _____ , as he makes his way through the streets, is a pleasant sound on a summer evening.

17. Since I was obeying all traffic regulations at the time that the accident occurred, I _____ responsibility for it.

18. Most religions rest on faith in a Supreme Being of _____ power and goodness.

19. Now that we have arranged a(n) _____ , we have the even harder job of making a real peace.

20. The Declaration of Independence's assertion that "all men are created equal" marked a new _____ in world history.

Synonyms   *From the words for this unit, choose the one that is most nearly **the same** in meaning as each of the following group of expressions. Write the word on the line given.*

1. rickety, unsteady; run-down, dilapidated   _____

2. endless, unlimited, inexhaustible   _____

3. a peddler, hawker, dealer, merchant   _____

4. to part company; to alienate   _____

5. financially sound, in the black   _____

6. mild, soothing; dull, insipid   _____

7. to wipe out, erase, expunge, efface   _____

8. unthinking repetition, mechanical routine   _____

9. long and boring, monotonous, tiresome _____

10. to look high and low, rummage, scour _____

11. a period, era, age _____

12. high-handed, overbearing, presumptuous _____

13. irritable, quarrelsome, cantankerous _____

14. a nook, recess _____

15. a cease-fire, truce _____

16. one's relatives; like, similar _____

17. to satisfy, indulge, humor; to delight _____

18. to increase, augment, fill out, supplement _____

19. to deny, disavow, disown, repudiate _____

20. innocent, wet behind the ears, "green" _____

Antonyms   From the words for this unit, choose the one that is most nearly **opposite** in meaning to each of the following groups of expressions. Write the word on the line given.

1. to bring together, reunite, reconcile _____

2. to admit, acknowledge, avow, confess _____

3. well built, well maintained, shipshape, trim _____

4. limited, restricted; measurable _____

5. to foster, promote; to create, bring into being _____

6. a buyer, purchaser, customer _____

7. meek, humble, modest, unassuming _____

8. even-tempered, slow to anger _____

9. bankrupt, flat broke, in the red _____

10. to disappoint, dissatisfy; to frustrate, thwart _____

11. harsh, irritating; pungent, spicy, piquant _____

12. unlike, dissimilar, contrasting _____

13. to lessen, diminish; to abbreviate, shorten _____

14. short and sweet; stimulating, interesting _____

15. sophisticated, knowing, urbane, suave, blasé _____

16. to spot-check, give the once-over _____

Choosing the Right Word *Encircle the **boldface** word that more satisfactorily completes each of the following sentences.*

1. Can anyone be so (**naive, irascible**) as to believe that all famous people who endorse products on TV actually use those products?

2. My next-door neighbor is a(n) (**tedious, arrogant**) chap, with a remarkable talent for boring me out of my wits.

3. We are now learning the hard way that our energy sources are not (**infinite, ramshackle**), and that we will have to use them carefully.

4. The business had been losing money for years, but under his careful management it finally reached a state of (**epoch, solvency**).

5. I (**ransacked, gratified**) my brain feverishly, but I was unable to find any way out of the difficulty.

6. I am willing to forgive you, but I can never (**obliterate, estrange**) from my mind the memory of your dishonesty.

7. He found a comfortable (**niche, rote**) for himself at a bank and worked there quite happily for the next 40 years.

8. What is important for the children is not a(n) (**infinite, rote**) recital of the Pledge of Allegiance but an understanding of what the words really mean.

9. Every week he meets with a small circle of (**bland, kindred**) souls whose greatest interest in life is the music of J.S. Bach.

10. The beginning of commercial television in the 1940s marked a new (**niche, epoch**) in the history of mass communications.

11. They claim to have "buried the hatchet," but I fear that they have only concluded a temporary (**kindred, armistice**) in their feud.

12. The spirit of the new law to protect consumers is not "Let the buyer beware," but rather "Let the (**vendor, epoch**) beware."

13. Rather than (**disclaim, gratify**) their religious faiths, many Catholics, Protestants, and Jews left Europe to settle in the New World.

14. Although Paul was furiously angry, he faced his accusers with a (**tedious, bland**) smile.

15. The job of the marriage counselor is to help (**kindred, estranged**) couples find a basis for settling their differences.

16. The excuse that he offered for his absence was so (**bland, ramshackle**) and improbable that it fell apart as soon as we looked into it.

17. You will learn that nothing is more (**amplifying, gratifying**) than to face a problem squarely, analyze it clearly, and overcome it successfully.

18. Over the years, the vigorous foreign policy that this country has pursued has greatly (**amplified, ransacked**) our role in world affairs.

19. It has always been typical of the (**armistice, arrogance**) of youth to assume that the older generation "has made a mess of things."

20. Whenever my supervisor gets into one of his (**bland, irascible**) moods, I know that I'm in for some heavy weather before the day is out.

Unit 15

Definitions

Note carefully the spelling, pronunciation, and definition of each of the following words. Then write the word in the blank space in the illustrative phase following.

1. **abyss**
   (ə 'bis)

   (*n.*) a deep or bottomless pit

   fall into the _____

2. **befall**
   (bi 'fôl)

   (*v.*) to happen, occur; to happen to

   let no evil _____ them

3. **crucial**
   ('krü shal)

   (*adj.*) of supreme importance, decisive, critical

   at the _____ moment

4. **dregs**
   (dregz)

   (*pl. n.*) the last remaining part; the part of least worth

   the _____ at the bottom of the pot

5. **embody**
   (em 'bäd ē)

   (*v.*) to give form to; to incorporate, include; to personify

   _____ his ideas in our plan

6. **exasperate**
   (eg 'zas pə rāt)

   (*v.*) to irritate, annoy, or anger

   _____ me with endless questions

7. **fiasco**
   (fē 'as kō)

   (*n.*) the complete collapse or failure of a project

   an embarrassing _____

8. **garnish**
   ('gär nish)

   (*v.*) to adorn or decorate, especially food; (*n.*) an ornament or decoration, especially for food

   used as a _____ for seafood

9. **heritage**
   ('her ə tij)

   (*n.*) an inheritance; a birthright

   the priceless _____ of civilization

10. **inert**
    (in 'ərt)

    (*adj.*) lifeless, unable to move or act; slow, inactive

    an _____ gas

11. **mercenary**
    ('mər sə ner ē)

    (*adj.*) acting or working for self-gain only; (*n.*) a hired soldier

    the shopkeeper's _____ attitude

12. **negligent**
    ('neg lə jənt)

    (*adj.*) marked by carelessness or indifference; failing to do what should be done

    charged with _____ driving

13. **oblivion**
    (ə 'bliv ē ən)

    (*n.*) forgetfulness, disregard; a state of being forgotten; an amnesty, general pardon

    rescued his plays from _____

14. **opus**
    ('ō pəs)

    (*n.*) an impressive piece of work (especially a musical composition or other work of art)

    piano sonata, _____ 2, No. 2

15

15. pallid
('pal id)

(*adj.*) pale, lacking color; weak and lifeless

a _____ complexion

16. parable
('par ə bəl)

(*n.*) a short narrative designed to teach a moral lesson

read the _____ of the lost sheep

17. rational
('rash ə nəl)

(*adj.*) based on reasoning; able to make use of reason; sensible, reasonable

a _____ explanation

18. reciprocal
(ri 'sip rə kəl)

(*adj.*) shared; involving give-and-take between two persons or things; working in both directions; (*math*) a number that, when multiplied by another number, gives 1

_____ trade agreements

19. stricture
('strik chər)

(*n.*) a limitation or restriction; a criticism; (*medicine*) a narrowing of a passage in the body

new _____ on press coverage

20. veneer
(və 'nēr)

(*n.*) a thin outer layer; the surface appearance or decoration; (*v.*) to cover with a thin layer

a thin _____ of fine walnut

Completing the Sentence

From the words for this unit, choose the one that best completes each of the following sentences. Write the word in the space provided.

1. The judge imposed a heavy fine on the _____ landlord who had failed to provide heat during the cold weather.

2. Would you like your new desk finished with a walnut, maple, or mahogany _____ ?

3. The story of the Prodigal Son is a(n) _____ that helps us understand problems and situations of present-day life.

4. The administration intends to propose legislation to cut back on customs duties and relax other _____ on foreign trade.

5. The old adage "I'll scratch your back if you'll scratch mine" aptly describes the kind of _____ arrangement he has in mind.

6. During her confinement in a Nazi concentration camp, she drained the cup of human suffering to the _____ .

7. My mother doesn't think that a plate of food is ready to serve unless she has _____ it with a sprig of parsley or a slice of tomato.

8. Since many composers don't publish their own works in the order they were written, _____ numbers often don't tell much about the date of composition.

9. In high school you will make many decisions _____ to your future, but determining what to wear to the prom isn't one of them.

10. To our dismay, Tom didn't get to his feet after being tackled on the play but lay _____ on the field.

11. Winston Churchill warned the English people that if they gave in to the Nazis, they would "sink into the _____ of a new Dark Age."

12. Of course Sid doesn't look well after his stay in the hospital, but a few days at the beach will take care of that _____ complexion.

13. A number of famous Roman emperors were clearly madmen for whose actions no _____ explanation can possibly be devised.

14. He was a famous novelist in his own day, but his work has now passed into _____ .

15. In no time at all, poor management turned what should have been a sure-fire success into a costly _____ .

16. Without pretending that he cared about the public welfare, he told us frankly that his interest in the project was purely _____ .

17. Astrologers claim that they can discover what will _____ a person by studying the movements of various heavenly bodies.

18. As we enter the third century of our nation's history, let us try to be worthy of our _____ of freedom!

19. The basic moral values of several religions are _____ in the brief code of laws known as the Ten Commandments.

20. Nothing _____ me more than people who play their radios, stereos, tape decks, or TV sets at high volume late at night.

Synonyms *From the words for this unit, choose the one that is most nearly **the same** in meaning as each of the following groups of expressions. Write the word on the line given.*

1. grasping, avaricious; a soldier of fortune _____

2. a work, composition, piece, oeuvre _____

3. motionless; inactive, sluggish, lethargic _____

4. a facing, overlay, façade; a pretense _____

5. to irritate, vex, try one's patience _____

6. mutual, give-and-take, quid pro quo _____

7. to incorporate, encompass; to personify _____

8. a restraint, restriction; a criticism   _____

9. a moral tale or fable, allegory   _____

10. decisive, critical, pivotal   _____

11. sensible, logical, reasonable   _____

12. a bottomless pit, chasm, gorge   _____

13. forgetfulness; obscurity, nothingness   _____

14. the grounds, lees, residue, leftovers   _____

15. colorless, bloodless, ashen; insipid   _____

16. careless, neglectful, remiss, derelict   _____

17. a failure, disaster, flop, bomb   _____

18. an inheritance, legacy; descent, pedigree   _____

19. to happen, occur, come to pass   _____

20. to embellish, decorate, gussy up   _____

Antonyms   *From the words for this unit, choose the one that is most nearly* **opposite** *in meaning to each of the following groups of expressions. Write the word on the line given.*

1. careful, attentive, conscientious   _____

2. to soothe, mollify; to please, delight   _____

3. unselfish, disinterested, altruistic   _____

4. ruddy, sanguine; racy, colorful   _____

5. mad, insane; illogical, absurd   _____

6. insignificant, inconsequential   _____

7. a complete success, triumph, hit   _____

8. vigorous, energetic; volatile; lively   _____

9. one-sided, unilateral   _____

10. a compliment, praise, accolade; a swelling   _____

11. fame, renown, celebrity   _____

12. a summit, promontory, pinnacle   _____

13. the upper crust, cream of the crop, elite   _____

14. the inner core, nucleus   _____

Choosing the Right Word — *Encircle the **boldface** word that more satisfactorily completes each of the following sentences.*

1. If our leadership is timid and (**crucial, inert**), we will never be able to solve the great problems that face us.

2. Since decent people would have nothing to do with him, he soon began to associate with the (**dregs, fiasco**) of society.

3. Underneath the (**veneer, oblivion**) of his polished manners and smooth talk, we recognized the simple country boy we had known in earlier years.

4. In this early novel of Dickens, we have an (**abyss, opus**) that gives us a wonderful picture of life in 19th-century England.

5. A West Point graduate, my uncle (**garnished, embodied**) all the qualities suggested by the phrase "an officer and a gentleman."

6. What a relief to turn from those (**pallid, negligent**) little tales to the lively, vigorous, earthy stories of Mark Twain.

7. After his crushing defeat in the election, the candidate returned to his hometown and disappeared into (**heritage, oblivion**).

8. Isn't it tragic that the religious groups fighting each other are separated by an (**opus, abyss**) of misunderstanding?

9. His constant chattering while I'm trying to do my vocabulary exercises (**exasperates, embodies**) me more than I can say.

10. "The heroism of these brave men and women speaks for itself," the Senator remarked, "and needs no (**oblivion, garnishing**)."

11. There are times when it is good to let your imagination run free, instead of trying to be strictly (**rational, crucial**).

12. Such familiar stories as "Little Red Riding Hood" are really (**parables, veneers**) that tell a child something about the conditions of human life.

13. Once the war had been won, the victors laid aside their high-minded ideals and became involved in a (**mercenary, pallid**) squabble over the spoils.

14. It's hard for us to admit that many of the misfortunes that (**garnish, befall**) us are really our own fault.

15. If you are (**negligent, inert**) about small sums of money, you may find that you will never have any large sums to worry about.

16. Any significant (**dregs, stricture**) of the passages leading to the heart will hinder the normal flow of blood to that organ and cause cardiac arrest.

17. The plan of the two schools to exchange members of their faculties proved to be of (**rational, reciprocal**) advantage.

18. Since he undertook that big job without any sound preparation, all of his ambitious plans ended in a resounding (**abyss, fiasco**).

19. Experience teaches us that many of the things that seemed so (**crucial, inert**) when we were young are really of no ultimate importance.

20. A descendant of one of the Founding Fathers of this country, she strove all her life to live up to her distinguished (**opus, heritage**).

Analogies   *In each of the following, encircle the item that best completes the comparison.*

1. arrogant is to **haughty** as
a. wry is to cynical
b. crucial is to decisive
c. steadfast is to treacherous
d. kindred is to dissimilar

2. pallid is to **complexion** as
a. forlorn is to size
b. pithy is to texture
c. reciprocal is to value
d. bland is to taste

3. veneer is to **thin** as
a. mountain is to flat
b. barn is to red
c. abyss is to deep
d. tide is to high

4. dovetail is to **together** as
a. attest is to apart
b. ransack is to together
c. estrange is to apart
d. disdain is to together

5. waif is to **forlorn** as
a. greenhorn is to naive
b. stoic is to irascible
c. vendor is to solvent
d. mercenary is to monetary

6. epoch is to **time** as
a. fiasco is to triumph
b. heritage is to occupation
c. oblivion is to number
d. niche is to place

7. impediment is to **speech** as
a. infinity is to space
b. gridlock is to traffic
c. telephone is to communication
d. critic is to stricture

8. foreboding is to **before** as
a. prelude is to after
b. epilogue is to before
c. hindsight is to after
d. finale is to before

9. amplifier is to **volume** as
a. clock is to time
b. generator is to temperature
c. thermostat is to quality
d. accelerator is to speed

10. irascible is to **patience** as
a. arrogant is to pride
b. haughty is to greed
c. naive is to youth
d. inert is to energy

11. steadfast is to **falter** as
a. stubborn is to yield
b. silly is to simper
c. kindred is to agree
d. bland is to loiter

12. dregs is to **bottom** as
a. veneer is to top
b. parable is to bottom
c. foreboding is to top
d. heritage is to bottom

13. garnish is to **salad** as
a. jet plane is to transportation
b. epic poem is to limerick
c. hood ornament is to car
d. department store is to consumer

14. solvent is to **bankrupt** as
a. humble is to haughty
b. imperative is to urgent
c. negligent is to frivolous
d. infinite is to timely

15. vendor is to **sell** as
a. waif is to malinger
b. author is to ransack
c. mercenary is to loiter
d. pirate is to plunder

16. pallid is to **unfavorable** as
a. naive is to favorable
b. pithy is to favorable
c. ramshackle is to favorable
d. rote is to favorable

17. tedious is to **bore** as
a. gratifying is to vex
b. pithy is to falter
c. trying is to exasperate
d. wry is to yawn

18. composer is to **opus** as
a. writer is to oeuvre
b. painter is to easel
c. actor is to stage
d. sculptor is to marble

116

Identification   *In each of the following groups, encircle the word that is best defined or suggested by the introductory phrase.*

1. one who treats people in a high-handed and scornful way
a. reciprocal   b. mercenary   c. irascible   d. arrogant

2. a simple story that has an important lesson for all of us
a. solvent   b. parable   c. niche   d. armistice

3. "You scratch my back, and I'll scratch yours."
a. reciprocal   b. infinite   c. rational   d. naive

4. fitting together like the pieces of a jigsaw puzzle
a. pithy   b. dovetail   c. wry   d. kindred

5. the peddler on the street corner or a major department store
a. veneer   b. fiasco   c. vendor   d. waif

6. the great work that occupied the last 2 years of the composer's life
a. impediment   b. dregs   c. enormity   d. opus

7. "When in Rome, do as the Romans do."
a. adapt   b. loiter   c. embody   d. attest

8. a funny story with a touch of bitterness
a. wry   b. negligent   c. forlorn   d. bland

9. "I had nothing to do with their plans to crash the party."
a. inert   b. arrogant   c. disclaim   d. simper

10. a noted critic's reservations about the quality of a new Broadway play
a. impediments   b. parables   c. fiascos   d. strictures

11. turn the house upside down searching for the key
a. estrange   b. ransack   c. exasperate   d. falter

12. so trusting that anyone can fool him
a. forlorn   b. mercenary   c. irascible   d. naive

13. the beautiful spirituals that have come down to us from earlier generations
a. heritage   b. armistice   c. falter   d. kindred

14. "I can bear witness to the truth of her statement."
a. befall   b. vilify   c. disclaim   d. attest

15. a bottleneck that is slowing up progress
a. oblivion   b. impediment   c. vendor   d. foreboding

16. "Everything that could possibly go wrong has gone wrong!"
a. rote   b. epoch   c. fiasco   d. dregs

17. the old gang hanging around the corner drugstore
a. ransack   b. loiter   c. simper   d. malinger

18. Pliocene, Miocene, or Oligocene
a. abyss   b. niche   c. kindred   d. epoch

19. the cherries and lemon twists people use to "gussy up" the drinks they serve
a. niches   b. vendors   c. garnishes   d. enormities

20. an easy job that's just right for him
a. plunder   b. niche   c. ransack   d. vaunt

Shades of Meaning *Read each sentence carefully. Then encircle the item that best completes the statement below the sentence.*

The enormity of the task of reconstructing Europe after World War II and the single-minded determination with which the U.S.A. went about the job still boggle the mind. **(2)**

1. In line 1 the word **enormity** most nearly means
a. heinousness   b. difficulty   c. immensity   d. atrocity

Since I seem to be the last leaf on the grapevine, such waifs of gossip as come my way are few and far between, out-of-date, and thoroughly unreliable. **(2)**

2. The best definition for the word **waifs** in line 1 is
a. tidbits   b. urchins   c. statements   d. rumors

Long experience has taught me that a gentle bit of ribbing is a guaranteed solvent for jittery nerves or cold feet in the clutch. **(2)**

3. The phrase **solvent for** in line 2 is best defined as
a. cause of   b. explanation for   c. component of   d. solution to

"While men believe in the infinite, some pools will be thought to be bottomless." (Thoreau, *Walden*) **(2)**

4. The best meaning for the phrase **the infinite** in line 1 is
a. an incalculable number   c. a supreme being
b. the idea of boundlessness   d. the limitless reaches of space

"The taper feebly lights the dregs of night
As up the stairs the weary scholar climbs." **(2)**
    (A.E. Glug, "The Art of Tilting at Windmills," 131–132)

5. In line 1 the word **dregs** most nearly means
a. heavy burden   c. last hours
b. least valuable parts   d. pitchy blackness

Antonyms *In each of the following groups, encircle the word or expression that is most nearly the **opposite** of the first word in **boldface type**.*

1. gratify
a. satisfy
b. destroy
c. displease
d. overtake

2. inert
a. dangerous
b. active
c. necessary
d. casual

3. loiter
a. cause
b. rush
c. annoy
d. promise

4. bland
a. important
b. proud
c. funny
d. exciting

5. estrange
a. joke
b. unite
c. arrange
d. threaten

6. solvent
a. sturdy
b. untrue
c. boasted
d. bankrupt

7. reciprocal
a. one-sided
b. self-centered
c. thoroughgoing
d. halfhearted

8. vilify
a. denounce
b. praise
c. embarrass
d. overturn

9. haughty	12. exasperate	15. irascible	18. attest
a. cruel	a. destroy	a. fearful	a. accept
b. pretty	b. soothe	b. good-natured	b. reject
c. low	c. waste	c. narrow	c. offer
d. humble	d. annoy	d. self-centered	d. disprove
10. forlorn	**13. kindred**	**16. negligent**	**19. steadfast**
a. homeless	a. smart	a. careful	a. kind
b. blithe	b. unrelated	b. selfish	b. slow
c. wealthy	c. disturbed	c. calm	c. wavering
d. woebegone	d. angry	d. thoughtless	d. pleased
11. ramshackle	**14. pallid**	**17. amplify**	**20. crucial**
a. quiet	a. shared	a. widen	a. mechanical
b. faded	b. fair	b. reduce	b. pivotal
c. wise	c. simple	c. abandon	c. flexible
d. sturdy	d. ruddy	d. remove	d. minor

Completing the Sentence   *From the following words, choose the one that best completes each of the sentences below. Write the word in the appropriate space.*

Group A

vaunted	foreboding	irascible	rote
impediment	crucial	garnish	oblivion
imperative	bland	ramshackle	armistice

1. Shakespeare spoke of the last stage of human lifetime as "second childhood and mere _____ ."

2. Let's call a(n) _____ in our quarrel so that we can work together for the Community Chest drive.

3. He is a skillful public speaker, but I have the impression that he is just repeating by _____ whatever his advisers tell him.

4. If you have prepared yourself properly for the exams, there is no need for a sense of _____ .

5. My boss never asks questions and rarely makes a declarative statement; the mood of his language is _____ .

Group B

obliterate	opus	stricture	fiasco
ransack	malinger	veneer	dregs
rational	infinite	embody	befall

1. Who knows what trouble and misfortune may _____ those inexperienced young people living alone in a big city!

2. A thin _____ of "fancy" manners could not hide the fact that Van was a crude and inconsiderate person.

R

3. When we saw Harry limping at first on his right foot, and the next day on his left, we realized that he was _____ .

4. Laura _____ all the qualities that we expect in a typical American high-school girl.

5. Although the play wasn't an outright hit, it wasn't a(n) _____ either.

Word Families

A. *On the line provided, write a **noun form** of each of the following words.*

EXAMPLE: solvent — **solvency**

1. amplify _____

2. infinite _____

3. embody _____

4. malinger _____

5. bland _____

6. estrange _____

7. exasperate _____

8. tedious _____

9. loiter _____

10. inert _____

11. pithy _____

12. naive _____

B. *On the line provided, write a **verb form** of each of the following words.*

EXAMPLE: foreboding — **forebode**

1. vendor _____

2. embodiment _____

3. negligent _____

4. rational _____

5. reciprocal _____

6. disclaimer _____

7. vilification _____

8. adaptable _____

9. impediment _____

10. gratification _____

**Filling
the Blanks**

*Encircle the pair of words that best complete the
meaning of each of the following sets of sentences.*

1. Though police officers in my neighborhood are sometimes accused of
_____ or otherwise lying down on the job, let me point out
that the diligence and efficiency with which they solve most cases clearly
_____ their overall devotion to duty.
   a. malingering . . . attests to   c. negligence . . . disclaims
   b. inertia . . . obliterates   d. steadfastness . . . dovetails with

2. "You don't need to address issues that will clearly have no effect on the
outcome of this election," the campaign manager told the candidate. "But
it is _____ for you to take a firm stand on those that may
prove _____ ."
   a. tedious . . . bland   c. gratifying . . . pallid
   b. naive . . . reciprocal   d. imperative . . . crucial

3. "All my critics claim that my support for human rights has never been
anything but halfhearted," the Senator remarked. "However, the record
clearly shows that I have been _____ in my commitment to
this great cause. Indeed, I take great pride in the fact that I have never
_____ or wavered in my allegiance to it."
   a. bland . . . malingered   c. inert . . . adapted
   b. steadfast . . . faltered   d. negligent . . . loitered

4. Acquiring a foreign language can be a particularly _____
chore because it involves so much memorization. If a person didn't have to
learn everything by _____ , the task would be a good deal
less time-consuming.
   a. foreboding . . . epoch   c. tedious . . . rote
   b. exasperating . . . niche   d. irascible . . . heritage

5. "Though I am certainly _____ that most critics gave my new
play rave reviews," the author remarked, "I can't help feeling a little hurt by
the _____ of those who panned it."
   a. vaunted . . . parables   c. estranged . . . enormities
   b. exasperated . . . disclaimers   d. gratified . . . strictures

6. Though most immigrants to this country have found it necessary to modify
or _____ the traditions they bring with them in order to meet
the needs of life in a new environment, few have totally abandoned the rich
_____ of their ancestors.
   a. adapt . . . heritage   c. plunder . . . veneer
   b. vilify . . . impediment   d. amplify . . . kindred

Cumulative Review Units 1–15

Analogies *In each of the following, encircle the letter of the item that best completes the comparison.*

1. disclaim is to **avow** as
a. muster is to amass
b. encroach is to abut
c. nullify is to ratify
d. bludgeon is to ravage

2. barter is to **trader** as
a. sell is to vendor
b. rehabilitate is to waif
c. endow is to recipient
d. cite is to author

3. crucial is to **pivotal** as
a. churlish is to personable
b. predominant is to subordinate
c. haughty is to willful
d. dire is to calamitous

4. nonentity is to **oblivion** as
a. celebrity is to renown
b. coward is to audacity
c. recluse is to popularity
d. laggard is to wisdom

5. predatory is to **plunder** as
a. stoical is to impunity
b. mercenary is to profit
c. naive is to perspective
d. retentive is to longevity

6. bland is to **caustic** as
a. gaunt is to emaciated
b. curt is to pithy
c. haggard is to ungainly
d. pallid is to ruddy

7. frugal is to **solvent** as
a. gingerly is to devoid
b. economical is to penniless
c. prodigal is to bankrupt
d. wanton is to wealthy

8. foreboding is to **premonition** as
a. acme is to pinnacle
b. citadel is to dungeon
c. vigil is to night
d. residue is to ingredient

9. unflagging is to **waver** as
a. steadfast is to falter
b. enterprising is to vie
c. fervent is to wallow
d. overbearing is to loiter

10. delve is to **mole** as
a. tether is to horse
b. ransack is to ferret
c. devise is to wolf
d. convey is to goat

11. elite is to **dregs** as
a. niche is to antics
b. bonanza is to windfall
c. fiasco is to plaudits
d. promontory is to abyss

12. cryptic is to **puzzle** as
a. negligent is to obey
b. tedious is to bore
c. veritable is to scoff
d. infinite is to exhaust

13. inert is to **volatile** as
a. aloof is to withdrawn
b. rational is to judicious
c. porous is to watertight
d. prone is to forthright

14. irascible is to **vex** as
a. jaunty is to anguish
b. impartial is to prejudice
c. impatient is to exasperate
d. disgruntled is to appease

15. sounds are to **discordant** as
a. times are to belated
b. sizes are to prodigious
c. agreements are to reciprocal
d. directions are to divergent

16. shiftless is to **malinger** as
a. dexterous is to fumble
b. conservative is to adapt
c. skittish is to cower
d. solicitous is to simper

17. arrogant is to **unassuming** as
a. blasé is to enthusiastic
b. ethical is to indiscriminate
c. menial is to servile
d. infinite is to ample

18. resolute is to **qualms** as
a. wry is to worries
b. frivolous is to ideas
c. pert is to duties
d. forlorn is to friends

19. venerate is to **vilify** as
a. dovetail is to converge
b. magnify is to minimize
c. obliterate is to preclude
d. attribute is to attest

20. parable is to **moral** as
a. sentence is to question mark
b. adage is to happy ending
c. joke is to punch line
d. stricture is to logical flaw

21. grapple is to **implement** as
a. tether is to machine
b. epitaph is to tombstone
c. bludgeon is to weapon
d. bolster is to utensil

22. turncoat is to **defect** as
a. collar is to chafe
b. scapegoat is to ostracize
c. idea is to obsess
d. quisling is to collaborate

Shades of Meaning   *Read each sentence carefully. Then encircle the item that best completes the statement below the sentence.*

Though gold and copper are highly tractable materials, iron is not because it requires extremely high temperatures to melt. **(2)**

1. The word **tractable** in line 1 most nearly means
a. malleable   b. docile   c. precious   d. dutiful

After a little over a decade of nonstop growth the economy suddenly began to falter and sink into depression. **(2)**

2. The best meaning for the word **falter** in line 2 is
a. hesitate   b. stammer   c. weaken   d. fluctuate

"I know that the opinions I hold are not popular," she replied, "but they are the result of much thought, and nothing will induce me to abdicate them." **(2)**

3. The word **abdicate** in line 2 is best defined as
a. disregard   b. disown   c. display   d. disinherit

I realized that my suggestion was not destined to "fly" when my boss wried up his face at the mere mention of it. **(2)**

4. The phrase **wried up** in line 2 most nearly means
a. washed   b. covered   c. turned   d. contorted

"For many of our princes (woe the while!)
Lie drowned and soaked in mercenary blood; **(2)**
So do our vulgar drench their peasant limbs
In blood of princes." (Shakespeare, *Henry V,* IV, vii, 76–79) **(4)**

5. The best meaning for **mercenary** in line 2 is
a. dearly purchased   c. of hired soldiers
b. relating to misers   d. grasping

The Nuremberg Trials set a precedent that makes it extremely unlikely that any government would in future consent to an act of oblivion for war criminals. **(2)**

6. The word **oblivion** in line 2 most nearly means
a. nothing   b. amnesty   c. forgetfulness   d. obscurity

**Filling
the Blanks**

*Encircle the pair of words that best complete the
meaning of each of the following sentences.*

1. The Civil Rights movement made significant advances when the Supreme
Court threw out the "separate but equal" _____ in effect
for years and _____ all sorts of unfair laws and practices
based on it.
   a. accord . . . asserted
   b. decree . . . perused
   c. stance . . . bolstered
   d. doctrine . . . invalidated

2. At no time in our history have Americans been so divided as during the
_____ of the Civil War, when a great many families had
_____ on both sides and "brother fought brother."
   a. epoch . . . kindred
   b. intrigue . . . mercenaries
   c. sequel . . . cronies
   d. enormity . . . jurisdiction

3. Though the actual fighting was brought to a full stop by a temporary
_____ , the war was not finally concluded until a more
_____ settlement was effected at the peace table.
   a. ruse . . . outlandish
   b. armistice . . . durable
   c. opus . . . conventional
   d. juncture . . . capacious

4. Sharks have been aptly described as "relentless feeding machines"
because their _____ appetites never seem to be
_____ .
   a. staid . . . appeased
   b. ample . . . regaled
   c. indiscriminate . . . stinted
   d. voracious . . . gratified

5. Delightful though they truly are, her personal _____ and
eccentricities are so pronounced that no _____ of manners
and polish can ever hope to mask them.
   a. tenets . . . milieu
   b. defects . . . crusade
   c. quirks . . . veneer
   d. enmities . . . residue

6. In Arthurian legend and romance, Sir Galahad is an idealized figure who
_____ purity, nobility, and all the other _____
associated with a virtuous knight, whereas Sir Lancelot is much more
human and consequently falls short of the mark.
   a. embodies . . . attributes
   b. proclaims . . . fallacies
   c. entails . . . epitaphs
   d. negates . . . repercussions

7. Before human beings _____ money, which first came into
use in Asia Minor during the 7th century B.C., goods were exchanged by
means of the _____ system, or trading in kind.
   a. imparted . . . quirk
   b. entailed . . . embargo
   c. defaced . . . decoy
   d. devised . . . barter

Final Mastery Test

I. Selecting Word Meanings *In each of the following groups, encircle the word or expression that is most nearly **the same** in meaning as the word in **boldface type** in the introductory phrase.*

1. came upon a **bonanza**
a. monster   b. problem   c. disaster   d. windfall

2. the **citadels** of power
a. drawbacks   b. trappings   c. strongholds   d. uses

3. traveled **incognito**
a. disguised   b. alone   c. luxuriously   d. safely

4. a **legendary** character
a. foreign   b. mythical   c. fascinating   d. historical

5. **audacious** plans
a. careless   b. successful   c. bold   d. unflagging

6. tries to appear **blasé**
a. calm   b. interested   c. knowledgeable d. bored

7. to **oust** the intruders
a. fight   b. greet   c. expel   d. discover

8. **cowered** in their cages
a. growled   b. slept   c. cringed   d. roared

9. **indiscriminate** slaughter
a. unreported   b. unplanned   c. unselective   d. unusual

10. **basked** in the limelight
a. reveled   b. hid   c. flourished   d. faded

11. **menial** jobs
a. well-paid   b. interesting   c. low-level   d. professional

12. **wallow** in the mud
a. roll   b. grow   c. play   d. work

13. **flaunt** their wealth
a. conceal   b. show off   c. enjoy   d. use

14. a **cryptic** reply
a. sensible   b. pleasing   c. hostile   d. puzzling

15. **divergent** roads
a. parallel   b. crossing   c. rough   d. separating

16. plans that go **awry**
a. amiss   b. slowly   c. forward   d. smoothly

17. a **curt** note
a. childish   b. humorous   c. brusque   d. courteous

18. to **devise** a method
a. discard   b. invent   c. borrow   d. explain

19. a **calamitous** fire
a. sudden   b. minor   c. devastating   d. brief

20. full of **quirks**
a. failures   b. peculiarities   c. ideas   d. mistakes

21. tried to **convey** my ideas
a. disclaim   b. amplify   c. express   d. defend

22. an **imperative** duty
a. essential   b. expensive   c. terrifying   d. burdensome

23. **kindred** languages
a. foreign   b. modern   c. ancient   d. related

24. a **forlorn** expression on his face
a. happy   b. woebegone   c. puzzled   d. surly

25. whatever may **befall** us
a. please   b. amuse   c. help   d. happen to

II. Synonyms   *In each of the following groups, encircle the two words or expressions that are most nearly* **the same** *in meaning.*

26. a. hover   b. articulate   c. muster   d. amass

27. a. bolster   b. plunder   c. grope   d. ravage

28. a. foreboding   b. stricture   c. premonition   d. unison

29. a. obsess   b. invalidate   c. assert   d. annul

30. a. waver   b. wallow   c. convey   d. falter

31. a. vex   b. ostracize   c. exasperate   d. rehabilitate

32. a. aghast   b. wanton   c. willful   d. exotic

33. a. facetious   b. overbearing   c. personable   d. arrogant

34. a. inaudible   b. crucial   c. pivotal   d. vaunted

35. a. nullify   b. proclaim   c. tether   d. negate

36. a. habituate   b. maim   c. incapacitate   d. loiter

37. a. pertinent   b. rational   c. relevant   d. abashed

38. a. aloof   b. prone   c. apt   d. predatory

39. a. steadfast   b. oblique   c. pithy   d. resolute

126

40.   a. sustain   b. belittle   c. minimize   d. venerate

III. Supplying Words in Context   *In each of the sentences below, write in the blank space the most appropriate word chosen from the following list.*

Group A

ensue	pallid	shiftless	proximity
evolve	purge	malinger	elite
ransack	embody	avail	vie
peruse	fend	estrange	ethical
endow	disdain	retentive	ornate

41. Unless he improves his _____ ways, he will not be successful at that job.

42. We _____ every room in the house hoping to find the missing book.

43. Before you fill out the job application, you should _____ the instructions carefully.

44. A riot may _____ if the crowd is not properly controlled.

45. How can the employers expect any one applicant for the job to _____ *all* the qualities they are seeking?

Group B

dexterous	finesse	solicitous	devoid
opus	levity	fallacy	scavenger
decoy	myriad	stoical	parry
disgruntled	waif	vilify	impending
glut	preclude	renown	vigil

46. Jane Addams won great _____ for her noble work to help people living in the slums.

47. The defense attorney remarked with satisfaction that the lack of solid evidence against her client would _____ his conviction.

48. With Larry serving as a(n) _____ to attract their attention, we managed to get away without their seeing us.

49. Of all the _____ woes of mankind, is there anything worse than a toothache?

50. The fans were _____ because they were convinced that their team had lost as the result of bad officiating.

FMT

IV. Word Pairs   *In the space provided before each of the following word pairs write:*

S — if the words are synonyms or near synonyms.
O — if the words are antonyms or near antonyms.
N — if the words are unrelated in meaning.

51. _____ haughty—unassuming   56. _____ haggard—gaunt

52. _____ regale—attest   57. _____ heritage—veneer

53. _____ deplore—rue   58. _____ pert—jaunty

54. _____ prodigal—frugal   59. _____ genial—churlish

55. _____ capacious—rote   60. _____ reconcile—estrange

V. Words Connected with History   *Some words that are used in connection with historical events are listed below. Write the appropriate word on the line next to each of the following descriptions.*

transition	decree	mercenary	embargo
trepidation	crusade	doctrine	reciprocal
armistice	epoch	turncoat	tenet
plebeian	scapegoat	repercussion	mediate

61. A term applied to Benedict Arnold because he sold out to the British during the American Revolution. _____

62. Any event or period of time that marks a major development in history. _____

63. A statement of ideas or policies, such as the one President Monroe issued in 1823, when he warned European governments to stay out of the New World. _____

64. A temporary halt in a war, such as the one that ended World War I in 1918. _____

65. The change that occurs when one President gives up power and the next President takes over. _____

66. A word applied to a trade agreement between the United States and Canada, in which each nation gives something that the other wants. _____

67. A great undertaking, such as the effort by Europeans to conquer the Holy Land in the 11th and 12th centuries. _____

68. Soldiers hired to fight for money—*e.g.*, the Hessians who served in the British army in the American Revolution. _____

69. To attempt to settle a dispute between two other parties, as the United States did in the Russo-Japanese War (1905).   _____

70. A policy of cutting off trade with other nations, as the United States did with France and England before the War of 1812.   _____

VI. Word Associations   *In each of the following, encircle the word or expression that best completes the meaning of the sentence or answers the question, with particular reference to the meaning of the word in* **boldface type**.

71. A speaker who is **tedious** is one who probably
  a. has prepared the talk carefully   c. deals with an important topic
  b. uses simple, direct language   d. speaks too long

72. Two ways in which you can **bludgeon** someone are with
  a. "sweet talk" and promises   c. courtesy and fair dealing
  b. a club and arguments   d. financial help and good advice

73. A **recluse** usually prefers to be
  a. out-of-doors   c. in a position of power
  b. in good company   d. alone

74. If you have **qualms** about something you have done,
  a. you are proud of yourself   c. you expect a reward
  b. your conscience is bothering you   d. you want to do the same thing again

75. When you say that an argument is **porous**, you mean that it
  a. is very strong   c. is well stated
  b. will hold up in a court of law   d. is full of logical "holes"

76. A person who serves as your **proxy** is
  a. a servant   c. one who acts in your place
  b. a medical specialist   d. a close friend

77. To be successful, a **mendicant** must master the art of
  a. lying   c. begging
  b. stealing   d. fencing

78. To be successful, a **vendor** should be good at
  a. accounting   c. carpentry
  b. salesmanship   d. diagramming sentences

79. If you are at the end of your **tether,** you are
  a. in good physical shape   c. sitting down
  b. ready to graduate   d. in a desperate situation

80. The word **teeming** would *not* be applied to
  a. the streets of a busy city   c. a jungle
  b. a heavy rainfall   d. an empty room

81. A **pseudonym** is most likely to be used by
  a. someone traveling incognito   c. a police officer
  b. a waif   d. a leading citizen of your community

82. Apparitions would be likely to play an important part in
a. your history book
b. ghost stories
c. a TV news program
d. a math examination

83. Which of the following would be most likely to **simper**?
a. your dentist
b. a foolish, self-conscious person
c. a judge sentencing a prisoner
d. a student taking a tough exam

84. People who have reached an **accord**
a. play musical instruments
b. are at the last stop of a bus line
c. are in agreement
d. work at similar jobs

85. Which of the following is outstanding for **longevity**?
a. a beautiful movie star
b. a 99-year-old person
c. an all-American halfback
d. a popular teacher

86. A **parable** would use a story to
a. take off weight
b. make arithmetical computations
c. get better gas mileage
d. clarify a moral idea

87. Someone who constantly **scoffs** might well be called a(n)
a. Doubting Thomas
b. Artful Dodger
c. Dapper Dan
d. Nervous Nelly

88. A **promontory** would be a good place to
a. play volleyball
b. let children play unattended
c. raise potatoes
d. look out to sea

89. An **avowed** pickpocket is one who
a. is helping the police
b. is exceptionally skillful
c. admits openly to his or her crimes
d. has never been caught and punished

90. Which of the following might be called **tawdry**?
a. a well-managed farm
b. a center for cancer research
c. a one-room schoolhouse
d. cheap, loud decorations

91. A **tractable** person is one who
a. can operate a tractor
b. owns a large tract of land
c. is easily influenced by others
d. is unbearably stubborn

92. The **residue** of a chemical experiment refers to
a. the equipment in the lab
b. what is left over after the experiment
c. the purpose of the experiment
d. the chemicals used

93. Which of the following would probably be **upbraided**?
a. a worn-out coat
b. an unruly student
c. a newborn baby
d. a heroic firefighter

94. From a friend with a **volatile** personality, you would expect
a. high moral standards
b. great stubbornness
c. interest in politics
d. sudden changes in mood

95. To do something without **stinting** is to be
a. careful
b. stingy
c. generous
d. in bad taste

96. The **jurisdiction** of a court refers to
  a. the kinds of cases it can decide
  b. where the court is located
  c. the qualifications of the judges
  d. the money needed to run the court

97. Which of the following would be likely to be **ungainly**?
  a. an Olympic gymnast
  b. an overweight ballet dancer
  c. a bankrupt businessman
  d. an eagle on the wing

98. Which of the following animals spends a great deal of time **delving** in the earth?
  a. a porcupine
  b. a beaver
  c. an otter
  d. a mole

99. Which of the following might aptly be classified as **wry**?
  a. a loaf of bread
  b. a sense of humor
  c. a twinge of conscience
  d. a cause of alarm

100. If your knowledge of words is **prodigious**, you will probably
  a. misuse many words
  b. have a small but useful vocabulary
  c. become an English teacher
  d. score close to 100% on this Final Test

Units 1–3

vers, vert—to turn

This root appears in **revert** (page 10), which means "to return, to go back to a previous, or lower, condition." Some other words based on the same root are listed below.

controversy	**inverse**	**traverse**	**vertiginous**
conversant	**pervert**	**verse**	**vice versa**
convertible	**reversal**		

From the list of words above, choose the one that corresponds to each of the brief definitions below. Write the word in the space at the right of the definition, and then in the illustrative phrase below the definition.

1. turned upside down or inside out; referring to a relationship in which one item increases as the other decreases (*"turned in"*) _____

since division is the _____ of multiplication

2. whirling or spinning; tending to make dizzy; affected by or suffering from dizziness _____

looked down from the _____ height

3. a line of poetry; poetic writing (*"a turning, as of a line"*) _____

recited the first _____ of her favorite poem

4. familiar by use or study; acquainted (*"turning with"*) _____

someone who is _____ with our problems

5. a lengthy dispute (*"a turning against"*) _____

refuse to take sides in the _____

6. able to be changed _____

bonds _____ into cash

7. to turn away from the right course; to lead astray, distort (*"thoroughly, utterly turned"*) _____

accused of _____ our system of justice

8. to travel across; to cross and recross; to extend over _____

_____ the countryside by bicycle

9. a change or overthrow; a change of fortune (usually for the worse), setback _____

the court's _____ of the decision

10. with the relation, order, or meaning reversed (*"the position being changed"*) _____

They dislike us, and _____ .

From the list of words on page 131, choose the one that best completes each of the following sentences. Write the word in the space provided.

1. During the heat wave we observed that there is a(n) _____ relationship between the temperature and the amount of work people can do.

2. The third baseman on our softball team often substitutes for the shortstop, and

   _____ .

3. What I like about the new sofa is that it is easily _____ into a bed in case we have overnight guests.

4. You should get along well in your new community since you already seem to be

   thoroughly _____ with local customs.

5. She claimed that the editors had _____ her thoughtful article on varsity football into an attack on the school team.

6. The train ride along the edge of the _____ mountain cliff brought on a sudden dizzy spell that left me quite woozy.

7. A string of unexpected setbacks and _____ had turned the happy-go-lucky young man into an embittered curmudgeon.

8. In its proposal, the traffic commission recommended an elevated superhighway to

   _____ the congested business district.

9. We made certain that we had many different kinds of foods at the picnic in order to

   avoid any _____ about who would be limited to what.

10. How many people can remember the title of the famous poem of which the opening

    _____ is " 'Twas the night before Christmas, when all through the house"?

Units 4–6

curr, curs, cour—to run

This root appears in **recourse** (page 31). The original meaning was "a running back to," but the word now means "a turning to for help or protection" or "a source of help." Some other words based on the same root are listed below.

concourse	current	incur	recur
courier	cursive	precursor	recurrent
currency	discourse		

From the list of words above, choose the one that corresponds to each of the brief definitions below. Write the word in the space at the right of the definition, and then in the illustrative phrase below the definition.

1. to meet with, run into; to bring upon oneself (*"run into"*) _____

   _____ many unnecessary debts

2. a crowd; a thoroughfare; a place where crowds gather ("*running together*")　　　　　　　　　　_____

　　join the _____ of people in the village square

3. a flow, movement; of the present time; in general use　　_____

　　the _____ issue of the school magazine

4. to talk; a conversation, long discussion on some topic　　_____

　　deliver a(n) _____ on drug abuse

5. a handwriting or printing style in which letters are joined together; flowing　　_____

　　children practicing _____ writing

6. a forerunner; that which precedes and shows the way　　_____

　　ancient Athens, the _____ of modern democracies

7. to happen again, be repeated ("*run again*")　　_____

　　thoughts that _____

8. a messenger, usually on urgent or official business　　_____

　　send the valuable documents by _____

9. occurring or appearing repeatedly; returning regularly　　_____

　　a(n) _____ theme

10. money in actual use; common acceptance　　_____

　　the name of the unit of _____ of Guatemala

From the list of words on page 132, choose the one that best completes each of the following sentences. Write the word in the space provided.

1. Try as he might, Daniel could not identify a pattern in the _____ nightmares he suffered.

2. I still do not know what I could have done to _____ their anger.

3. "Will you please bring us up to date," the reporter asked pointedly, "by telling us

　　some of the _____ measures being planned to fight pollution."

4. The pound is the basic unit of _____ in Great Britain.

5. The architect planned a huge _____ in front of the City Hall as an open area where the citizens could gather.

6. We listened in interest as the veteran player _____ on the relative greatness of former basketball superstars.

7. In recent years we have seen a proliferation of _____ services specializing in the airborne transport of documents.

8. Do not wait until the sharp pains _____ ; see the doctor now!

9. The printer recommended a(n) _____ typeface to impart an elegant handwritten quality to the invitation.

10. The chilly autumn breeze was a(n) _____ of the cold weather to come.

Units 7–9

cap, capt, cept, cip—to take

This root appears in **capitulate** (page 63). The word originally meant "to be taken," but now has the meaning "to surrender, give in." Some other words based on the same root are listed below.

anticipate	**concept**	**incipient**	**receptacle**
caption	**deceptive**	**intercept**	**reception**
captivate	**exceptionable**		

From the list of words above, choose the one that corresponds to each of the brief definitions below. Write the word in the space at the right of the definition, and then in the illustrative phrase below the definition.

1. a social gathering; the manner of receiving (*"act of taking"*) _____

plan a(n) _____ for the new principal

2. open or liable to exception; objectionable _____

rebuked for his _____ behavior

3. to realize beforehand, foresee; to expect; to act so as to prevent _____

_____ his opponent's next move

4. a title, description, or explanation accompanying an illustration; a movie or TV subtitle _____

read the _____ under the cartoon

5. to check, stop, or interrupt the progress or course of _____

_____ the message before it could be delivered

6. a container _____

many convenient _____ for the trash

7. to charm, fascinate _____

a tale to _____ the imagination

8. in an early stage, just beginning (*"being taken into"*) _____

nurse a(n) _____ cold

9. a general notion or idea, thought _____

have a(n) _____ of the actual size of the universe

10. intended or apt to deceive, misleading _____

give a(n) _____ impression

From the list of words on page 134, choose the one that best completes each of the following sentences. Write the word in the space provided.

1. I found the author's tasteless slurs almost as _____ as the gross prejudice they betrayed.

2. I hope she realizes why I gave her such a cool _____ when she finally returned my telephone call.

3. The local police are investigating the newspaper ads that angry customers claimed were _____ and misleading.

4. The _____ on the desk contains the letters that require immediate attention.

5. The good looks and ready wit of the performer quickly _____ the audience.

6. We had expected a convincing win, but the margin of victory was even greater than we had _____ .

7. Many opera houses now _____ foreign-language operas with "supertitles" to provide a running translation of what is being sung.

8. Alice is so worried about her health that she thinks the slightest cough is a sign of _____ pneumonia.

9. Phil _____ so many passes during the game that he almost seemed to know in advance what the passer's next moves would be.

10. I regret to say that he has no _____ of how much trouble he has put us to.

Units 10–12

ven, vent—to come

This root appears in **conventional** (page 81). Literally, the word means "referring to or resulting from a coming together." It now has the meaning "customary, familiar, lacking in originality." Some other words based on the same root are listed below.

adventurous	**eventful**	**intervene**	**revenue**
circumvent	**eventual**	**inventive**	**venue**
convene	**eventuate**		

From the list of words above, choose the one that corresponds to each of the brief definitions below. Write the word in the space at the right of the definition, and then in the illustrative phrase below the definition.

1. good at making or thinking up new ideas or things; imaginative _____

fortunate to have a(n) _____ mind

2. full of events or incidents; important   _____

a(n) _____ evening

3. the place where a crime or cause of legal action occurs; a locality from which a jury is called and in which a trial is held; the scene or locale of any action or event   _____

request a change in _____

4. happening at an unspecified time in the future, ultimate   _____

foresaw a(n) _____ improvement

5. full of danger; fond of taking risks   _____

engage in a(n) _____ voyage into space

6. to assemble, come together; to call together   _____

on the day that our club regularly _____

7. to result; to come about ("to come out")   _____

regardless of what will _____

8. income; the income of a government; the yield from property or investment   _____

_____ from taxes

9. to get around or avoid; to defeat, overcome   _____

_____ the storm by flying further west

10. to come between; to enter to help settle a dispute   _____

refuse to _____ in the fight

From the list of words on page 135, choose the one that best completes each of the following sentences. Write the word in the space provided.

1. The rejected aliens searched for a way to _____ the law that kept them from staying in our country.

2. The _____ she receives from her investments is not sufficient to support her taste for luxury.

3. The coaches _____ before the battling players could seriously hurt themselves.

4. The principal quickly ordered all students to _____ in the school auditorium to prepare for the coming emergency.

5. His "big news" was about nothing more _____ than catching a five-pound bluefish.

6. The _____ of the political gathering was carefully chosen so as to guarantee a friendly audience.

7. I cannot accept the theory that predicts the _____ end of all life on Earth.

8. The captain of a modern nuclear-powered submarine must be more than just a(n)

_____ explorer.

9. I am positive that his _____ mind will come up with something more interesting than a better kind of mousetrap.

10. So far, the governor's campaign against pollution has _____ in nothing more than a formal report on the problem.

Units 13–15

fect, fic, fy—to make

This root appears in **amplify** (page 105), "to make bigger, increase." Some other words based on the same root are listed below.

beneficial	**confectionery**	**disinfect**	**exemplify**
certify	**defective**	**edify**	**personify**
clarify	**deify**		

From the list of words above, choose the one that corresponds to each of the brief definitions below. Write the word in the space at the right of the definition, and then in the illustrative phrase below the definition.

1. to make a god of; to worship as a god   _____

_____ their leader

2. candy; used in making candy   _____

a recipe that requires a pound of _____ sugar

3. to be the embodiment of; to represent the qualities of   _____

a woman who _____ kindness

4. to instruct so as to encourage intellectual, moral, or spiritual improvement   _____

a sermon that _____

5. to be an example of; show by example   _____

_____ the best in our group

6. to cleanse of infection by destroying disease germs   _____

use fluorine gas to _____ the clothing

7. to make clear or easier to understand   _____

asked to _____ her statement

8. favorable, helpful, producing good (*"making good"*)   _____

_____ to plants

9. to guarantee; to declare true or correct (*"make certain"*)   _____

_____ his signature on the check

10. faulty, not perfect, not complete   _____

replace the _____ part

From the list of words on page 137, choose the one that best completes each of the following sentences. Write the word in the space provided.

1. I'd advise liberal use of soap and water to _____ everything that the scarlet-fever victim had touched in this room.

2. Stained-glass windows were originally intended to _____ illiterate worshipers with pictorial depictions of Bible stories and parables.

3. Since 1947, the Japanese have regarded their emperor as a mere mortal rather than as a(n) _____ person.

4. Many contemporary medical experts agree that moderate exposure to the rays of the sun is _____ to one's health.

5. Instead of repeating your confusing remark over and over again, why don't you try to _____ it for us?

6. This disorganized mess _____ what can happen when we rush into a project without having a definite plan worked out and agreed on in advance.

7. Tomorrow, I plan to return to the manufacturer the electric broiler that proved to be

_____ .

8. The officials of the bank will have to _____ this check before we can accept it.

9. The flavored lozenges taste more like _____ than medicine.

10. To me, the statue of Venus de Milo _____ my idea of feminine beauty.

Index

The following tabulation lists all the basic words taught in the various units of this workbook, as well as those introduced in the *Vocabulary of Vocabulary* and *Building with Word Roots* sections. The number after each item indicates the page on which it is introduced and defined, but the word may also appear in exercises on later pages.